How
the Qur'an
Interprets
the Bible

How the Qur'an Interprets the Bible

COMPARING ISLAMIC, JEWISH, AND CHRISTIAN SCRIPTURES

John Kaltner
Christopher G. Frechette

Paulist Press
New York / Mahwah, NJ

Cover images: border image © Checco/Dreamstime.com; background image by Depositphotos/EnginKorkmaz
Cover design by Sharyn Banks
Book design by Lynn Else

Library of Congress Cataloging-in-Publication Data
Names: Kaltner, John, author. | Frechette, Christopher G., author.
Title: How the Qur'an interprets the Bible : comparing Islamic, Jewish, and Christian scriptures / John Kaltner, Christopher G. Frechette.
Description: New York : Paulist Press, [2020] | Includes bibliographical references and index. | Summary: "The Bible and the Qur'an are arguably the most frequently cited and most misunderstood books in history, and the relationship between them is often discussed but regularly misconstrued. This book introduces readers to the Qur'an by exploring how Islamic as well as Jewish and Christian scriptures convey meaning by drawing on traditions about some of the most well-known characters found in both texts"— Provided by publisher.
Identifiers: LCCN 2019029367 (print) | LCCN 2019029368 (ebook) | ISBN 9780809153992 (paperback) | ISBN 9781587687723 (ebook)
Subjects: LCSH: Qur'an—Relation to the Bible. | Abrahamic religions.
Classification: LCC BP134.B4 K348 2020 (print) | LCC BP134.B4 (ebook) | DDC 297.1/226—dc23
LC record available at https://lccn.loc.gov/2019029367
LC ebook record available at https://lccn.loc.gov/2019029368

ISBN 978-0-8091-5399-2 (paperback)
ISBN 978-1-58768-772-3 (e-book)

Published by Paulist Press
997 Macarthur Boulevard
Mahwah, New Jersey 07430
www.paulistpress.com

Printed and bound in the
United States of America

Contents

Introduction

F ew people would dispute that the Bible and the Qur'an are at the top of the list of the best-selling books of all time. Less recognized, even among people who follow the religions associated with them, is that the Bible and the Qur'an share much in common. Not only do certain characters appear in both, but the Bible and the Qur'an also both include later traditions that interpret prior traditions about those characters for distinctive religious purposes. This book will uncover significant similarities and differences between a number of such interpretive traditions. Focusing mainly on how the Qur'an interprets biblical traditions, it will draw attention to differences and similarities among qur'anic interpretations as well as between them and biblical interpretations. In this way, it will highlight how the Islamic text presents its own distinct vision of the traditions for its own purposes, as do biblical texts for their purposes.

The Recitation

The word *Qur'an* (also spelled Koran) is an Arabic term that means "recitation." This gets at a key aspect of the text—it is meant to be proclaimed orally and not simply read silently. The first person to proclaim the Qur'an was the Prophet Muhammad (570–632 CE), who lived in the western part of what is today Saudi Arabia. According to Muslim tradition, sometime in the year 610 he began to receive a series of revelations from God (*allāh*)[1] that continued over the rest of his life, and the Qur'an is an accurate

1

record of the revelations he received during that twenty-two-year period.

At just over six thousand verses, the Qur'an is approximately the same length as the New Testament. It is divided into 114 chapters that are arranged by length, with the longest ones coming at the beginning of the book and the shortest at its end. Scholars have determined that the earliest revelations Muhammad received were usually quite short, and so if one would like to get a general sense of the chronological development of the text, it should be read backward. Each of the chapters of the Qur'an has a title that usually refers to some person, theme, or word within it, and Muslims commonly refer to a chapter by its name. One can also identify a chapter by its number, and that is the approach adopted here.

The stories that the Qur'an has in common with the Bible are an important part of it, but they are just one component of a very complex text. The genres and styles of writing it contains are many and varied, and it is important to keep that issue in mind so as to avoid the mistaken belief that the present book gives a thorough and complete sense of Islamic scripture. In order to fill in the picture and gain an appreciation of its complexity, it is necessary to read as much of the Qur'an as one can. It is also important to remember that the Qur'an is not the only text of significance for Muslims. Other sources from which they draw guidance include the sayings of the Prophet Muhammad (*ḥadīth*), biographical accounts of his life, and collections of stories about the previous prophets (including the ones treated in this book). Nonetheless, "the Recitation" is the most sacred text for all Muslims because they believe it perfectly preserves God's message to humanity.

Although reading the Qur'an in translation affords one a basic knowledge of its contents, the only readers who are able to experience the Qur'an in its original form are those who know Arabic. Others cannot fully appreciate one of the most important features of the text—its poetic nature. Virtually every verse in each chapter ends with the same or nearly the same sound, and this creates an aural effect that is impossible to reproduce in another language. Of course, one can gain some sense of this dimension by listening to the text through a recording. But without knowledge of Arabic, the powerful interplay of sound and meaning is lost. This is such an essential component of the text that Islamic theology

2

holds that a translation of the Qur'an is not really the Qur'an but only an interpretation of it. Its poetic form relates directly to the meaning of the book's title and explains why "the Recitation" is a composition that is meant to be heard.

Islam teaches that the Qur'an is not the first time God delivered that message to people. Like Judaism and Christianity, Islam affirms the existence of only one God. Throughout history the deity has spoken to humanity through a series of individuals referred to in the text as prophets and messengers. Most of the people mentioned in the Qur'an who played these roles are familiar to readers of the Bible. Abraham, Moses, David, Solomon, Jonah, and Jesus are just a few of the biblical figures among the nearly three dozen prophets/messengers in Islamic scripture. According to Islamic teaching, each of these individuals brought the same message to humanity—that they should submit themselves to the will of God. In some cases, as with Moses and the Torah, and with Jesus and the gospel, the message took written form. The Qur'an maintains that those previous scriptures were somehow changed by the followers of the earlier prophets so that they no longer accurately presented God's message. Because of this distortion a final messenger, Muhammad, was sent by God to deliver the correct version of the message in the form of the Qur'an. The Arabic word for submission (*islām*) was the term used to describe that message, and one who surrenders oneself to the divine will is referred to as a submitter (*muslim*). The qur'anic versions of the traditions discussed in this book are therefore considered by Muslims to be the forms of those traditions that God originally intended for humanity.

Getting Your Bearings

A number of considerations about the Qur'an and the Bible are important to grasp at the outset. This is particularly the case for readers who have good knowledge of the Bible's contents. The Qur'an is both similar to and different from the Jewish and Christian scriptures, and reading familiar stories that are told in a different way can be an unsettling, even troubling, experience for some. Keeping the following points in mind might help to make the differences between the two texts less jarring and confusing.

This book presumes the perspective of many Christian communions, including Roman Catholics and many Protestant communions other than fundamentalists, that understanding the way in which humans wrote biblical texts helps to understand their religious meaning. In the ancient world, Jews, Christians, and Muslims, like many of their neighbors from other cultures and religious perspectives, wrote new religious texts to address their own situations in ways that included or adapted prior traditions that they received and for which they had great respect. This book uses the concept of interpretation in two ways. We mainly focus on how the ancients wrote new religious texts by interpreting old ones, that is, by drawing on traditional characters and stories to convey meaning—often multiple layers of meaning. As the Qur'an was written centuries after the youngest books of the Bible and in an environment of contact with Jews and Christians, it is easy to grasp that in referring to biblical characters the Qur'an generally reflects some awareness of narrative biblical traditions. It presents them for its own purposes by highlighting certain details or introducing details lacking in the biblical narrative. Additionally, we will discuss how scholars and other readers of the Qur'an and the Bible interpret the texts contained in them—that is, we will attempt to understand the meaning those texts were intended to communicate.

The Bible and Qur'an differ in that while the Qur'an is a single composition, the Bible is a collection of separate books. Moreover, many biblical books show evidence of coming together over time, during which those who preserved the traditions edited them into what became a given book's final form, which in many cases even preserves traditions that in some respects do not agree with each other. For instance, the Genesis account of the flood preserves two different traditions that do not agree on certain details, like the number of animals that God instructs be loaded into the ark.[2] Some groups of biblical books, like the Pentateuch—the first five books of the Bible, which Jews call the Torah—show signs that the books were edited into a unity while preserving multiple perspectives. While many biblical books share common themes, one may also find—within a given book and across different books—perspectives that are in tension with each other. The Qur'an, by contrast, although it also reflects multiple prior traditions, including

4

Introduction

some that involve biblical characters, represents a much more homogenous theological perspective.

A fundamental difference between Islam and Christianity concerns the manner in which each religion understands its originating figure in relation to its scriptures. Muslims understand Muhammad as a man, the final prophet sent by God with a definitive message about God's mercy and about how to live rightly and submit to God completely. Muslims believe that Muhammad recorded the Qur'an perfectly according to God's instruction, but Christians do not claim that Jesus wrote any of the books of the New Testament. Its twenty-seven books were written roughly between twenty and seventy years after Jesus died. For the early Christians who wrote those books, the teachings of Jesus of Nazareth about God and how to live in relationship with God and with each other were important, but Jesus was not simply a man who died after having taught God's message. They claimed through faith to encounter him in their lives as the risen Jesus, and the variety of texts that they wrote and that eventually were collected in the New Testament interpret Jesus in ways that integrate two basic elements. On the one hand, the writers wanted to pass on faithfully the traditions that they received from his first disciples about Jesus's life and teaching, and about his death and resurrection. On the other hand, their primary purpose was not to record past events and teachings for their own sake, but in order to give witness to believers' ongoing experience of the risen Jesus's powerful, yet mysterious, presence in their own lives. For the early Christians, the human Jesus who had lived, taught, and died was the same person as the risen Jesus whom they encountered. In writing the Gospels and other texts, they sought to help their communities and others to encounter him in faith through reflection and prayer, and especially communal worship.

Jesus and Muhammad play very different roles for the communities associated with them, and so it would be a mistake to think of them as functional equivalents, as Christians sometimes do. Encountering the risen Jesus in faith led early Christians to understand him as divine; for them, encountering him was an encounter with God (see chapter 1). Eventually, this experience led them to articulate the doctrine of the incarnation, that God took human form in Jesus, and the doctrine of the Trinity, that

5

one God exists in the persons of Father (Creator), Son (Jesus), and Holy Spirit (who enables faith). Thus, for Christians Jesus provides access to God. This is not the way Muslims view Muhammad, who was a human being and nothing more. The role that Jesus plays in Christianity is actually closer to that of the Qur'an in Islam; for Muslims, the message that Muhammad brought to his community reveals the divine will. Islam teaches that a book rather than a person provides the connecting link between God and humanity. For Christians, their scriptures (Old Testament and New Testament) are a privileged medium through which to encounter the risen Jesus, and through him, God.

The New Testament writers, like many early Christians, believed that Jesus had come from God according to the Jewish scriptures, and so they used those texts creatively to capture various dimensions of what it means to live in relationship with God and with the risen Jesus, whom they identified as Savior, Messiah/Christ, and Son of God. These titles identify Jesus as fulfilling the longing of Jews living under the oppression of the Greek and Roman empires for a divinely sent successor to King David who would save them from that oppression. The titles *Christ* and *Messiah* translate Greek and Hebrew words, respectively, that mean the same thing, "anointed." In ancient Israel, kings were anointed with oil to mark their special, divinely designated status.[3]

In the ancient world, an important aspect of religious traditions that gave them authority was their antiquity. That Christians refer to the Jewish scriptures as the Old Testament is not to consider it outdated, but to reverence the value of those texts in relationship to their belief in Christ. Each of the nine chapters in this book that treat characters from Jewish scriptures will discuss passages from the New Testament that interpret those characters in ways that express something about Christian belief in Jesus. In the discussion, we will generally refer to the Jewish scriptures and Christian Old Testament as the "Hebrew Bible."

Given the complex way in which the biblical books came into existence, further clarification is in order. For each character treated here, the Bible contains at least one substantial narrative tradition in addition to brief references, most of which were written later than those narratives. All of these texts, both longer narratives and brief references, interpret those characters in some way. On the one hand, it may be easy to grasp how the obviously later biblical traditions, such as those in the New Testament, are interpreting biblical characters from earlier Jewish traditions. On the other hand, even stories that occur earlier in sequence in the Bible (e.g., those in Genesis) show signs that they were crafted from prior traditions; the biblical writers sought to convey meaning by what they included and how they told the story. In both the lengthy narratives and the brief references we will see how the biblical writers are interpreting the characters for their own theological purposes. Although this book focuses primarily on how the Qur'an interprets biblical traditions about the characters, the discussion generally includes some comparison with how the biblical text also interprets those characters. In some cases (e.g., Moses and the golden calf tradition in chapter 6), the way the biblical text is telling the story to address a specific situation or with a specific perspective receives substantial attention.

The traditions shared by the Qur'an and the Bible are never told in the exact same way. In fact, in some cases the differences between them are much more obvious than the similarities. This is so because the Islamic text often attempts to highlight a theme or dimension of a tradition that is downplayed or perhaps not even present in the biblical text. Sometimes this indicates an effort to make the story more Islamic. For example, in some cases the theme of submission is an important part of the Islamic version of a tradition, while it is completely missing from the biblical one. Moreover, many qur'anic accounts of a tradition stress God's mercy because it is such a significant aspect of the Muslim understanding of the deity.

The Qur'an sometimes contains multiple versions of a tradition for which the Bible presents only one. Furthermore, when those qur'anic passages are compared to one another, there can be significant differences among them. This gets at a subtle but key distinction between the Qur'an and the Bible. As already mentioned, the lengthier parts of the Bible that treat the figures discussed in this book are written in prose, and they present narrative accounts of the lives, or parts of the lives, of individuals. The reader therefore encounters them as stories that relate a series of events that all fit together into a larger overall narrative. For example, the cycle of stories about Jacob (who is renamed "Israel") in

Genesis 25—49 describes various episodes in his life beginning with his birth and ending with his death.

This is typically not the way the Qur'an presents these traditions. It contains very few lengthy passages that treat the life of a person in some detail. The treatment tends to be much briefer and to focuses on only one event in the person's life. Even when it is a bit longer, the Qur'an's discussion of a person's life is usually more of a sketch with few details. The Islamic text also commonly moves on to another character after treating only briefly the previous one, who is often then mentioned again in other passages. For example, in the Qur'an Jacob is mentioned by name sixteen times, but those occurrences are found in passages that are only a verse or two in length in about ten different chapters. Its contents are arranged this way because the Qur'an usually cites an individual in order to teach a lesson or to make a point, and it is less concerned with presenting a narrative that provides a fuller account of the person's life story. Therefore, only that part of the person's life that helps to make the point or illustrate the lesson is mentioned in the text. This is also why the Qur'an sometimes contains different versions of the same tradition—each one attempts to highlight a different theme or teach a distinct lesson. We will pay attention to a similar way later biblical texts, especially in the New Testament, present characters known from prior Jewish tradition by making a brief reference to a character in order to make a theological point.

A related difference between how the Bible and the Qur'an present the characters treated in this book is that while the Bible contains at least one substantial narrative for each character, the Qur'an does not. Where one might expect the Islamic text to present a fuller narrative—for instance, the first time it mentions the character—it may contain significant narrative gaps regarding the events of stories, the motivations of characters, or what is said between them. At times it is difficult to gain a complete sense of a tradition unless the reader knows the biblical account and is able to fill in the gaps with the details provided in its version. This is probably the reason why the Qur'an account is relatively sparse—the lack of detail suggests that its original audience was quite familiar with the tradition being presented, and so there was no need to include all the details. The precise form of the fuller traditions that are reflected in the Qur'an is not completely clear, and it is an issue that scholars continue to debate. Although absence of evidence here is not conclusive, that there is no evidence for a translation of the Bible into Arabic until the eighth century suggests that the Qur'an's original audience may not have had access to biblical traditions written in their native language. It is, however, likely that they would have been familiar with them through versions of the traditions that were circulating orally.

What to Expect

Each of the following ten chapters discusses how a set of biblical characters is interpreted in the Qur'an in ways that are both similar to and different from how the Bible interprets them. Initial attention goes to one or more Qur'an passages that are related to the characters, exploring the interpretive process at work. Discussion of the qur'anic passages generally includes comparison with how substantial biblical narratives present the characters. While headings may distinguish sections that focus more on either comparing or interpreting, in actuality, the two activities are usually intermingled to some degree. Focus then turns to additional biblical passages, in most cases brief New Testament references, that engage in interpretation of the characters. For passages from both the Qur'an and the Bible, the discussion will demonstrate how certain details indicate particular perspectives or theological purposes in the text.

Because a grasp of how the New Testament interprets Jesus is so fundamental for understanding how it interprets characters from the Hebrew Bible, Mary and Jesus are taken up in the first chapter. Subsequent chapters take up characters from the Hebrew Bible in the order in which they appear in its core narrative (i.e., the story as it unfolds from Genesis through 2 Kings), with the exception of Job and Jonah. As their narratives are not part of that core narrative, Job and Jonah are taken up in the final two chapters.

Non-Muslims sometimes criticize the Qur'an for presenting biblical characters differently than they occur in biblical narratives. Ironically, however, we will see that such reinterpretations had already been legitimated and canonized by Jewish and Christian communities many centuries before the appearance of Islam's sacred text.

The present book is introductory, and readers may be interested in more information on any number of topics. Rather than including suggested resources in notes throughout the volume, the book concludes with a list of resources for further reading organized by topic.

CHAPTER 1

Mary and Jesus

The Qur'an displays some familiarity with the New Testament, but it contains much less material related to the New Testament than to the Hebrew Bible. The New Testament characters that the Islamic text mentions by name are Jesus, his mother Mary, John (known as "the Baptist" in Christianity), and John's father Zachariah,[1] whom the Gospel of Luke identifies as the husband of Elizabeth, a descendant of Aaron (priest and brother of Moses) and a relative of Mary. In addition, the Qur'an refers to unnamed disciples of Jesus several times (3:52–53; 5:111–15; 61:14). Two possible explanations emerge for this relative lack of information. The New Testament mentions fewer individuals who might be seen as predecessors to Muhammad and so help to legitimate his role as a prophet. In addition, the early Muslim community might have been less familiar with Christianity and its scriptural traditions than it was with Judaism. Scholars continue to debate the issue of how familiar the early Muslim community was with the New Testament and traditions associated with it. As discussed in this chapter, Christian claims regarding Jesus's divinity and the Trinity were known, but the precise means by which they were communicated remains uncertain.

The Islamic understanding of Jesus presents some unique theological and interreligious challenges because the Qur'an does something regarding him that it does not do in its interpretation of Hebrew Bible characters and stories—it flatly denies central Christian beliefs about Jesus. As discussed in the introduction, Muslims understand Muhammad as a man who was God's definitive prophet, while Christians—including those who wrote the New Testament—understand Jesus not merely as a man who taught God's message and died. A further central aspect of Christian belief about Jesus is not accepted by Muslims: that Jesus was raised from the dead and is present with believers through faith in mysterious and powerful ways, enabling them to be in right relationship with God.

The latter part of this chapter addresses the Qur'an's denial of two central Christian beliefs: that Jesus is a person of the divine Trinity, the Son of God; and that as God he became fully human. The earlier part of the chapter considers the Islamic text's presentation of the story of the announcement to Mary that she will give birth to Jesus, a story that the Qur'an treats in two different places.

A Birth and Two Birth Announcements

In the Qur'an, most women are mentioned by title, like the Queen of Sheba, or by their relationship to men, like the wife of Joseph's master in Egypt. Mary is the only woman mentioned by name, and chapter 19 of the text is named after her. The Qur'an refers to her in about seventy verses distributed among seven chapters. In chapter 3 it blends the story of Zachariah and John with that of Mary and Jesus, and in chapter 19 it recounts one after the other. Versions of the story of Jesus's birth appear in the Gospels of Matthew and Luke, and the Qur'an's presentation of it has more in common with the latter, the only one that includes the birth story of John the Baptist. The following discussion divides the story in chapter 3 of the Qur'an into three segments.

MARY'S BIRTH

The story begins with a description of Mary's birth, which is not described in the New Testament.

35 'Imran's wife said, "My Lord, I have vowed to You that what is in my womb will be dedicated to Your service.

Accept it from me, for You are the one who hears and the one who knows." [36]When she brought forth the child, she said, "My Lord, I have given birth to a female,"— but God knew what she had brought forth, for the male is not like the female—"and I have named her Mary. I place her and her offspring under Your protection from Satan, the cursed one." (Q 3:35–36)[2]

The New Testament does not identify Mary's parents, but in Christian tradition they have the names Joachim and Anne. The Qur'an calls her father 'Imran, which is the same name Moses's father has in Jewish extrabiblical sources. Mary's mother, unnamed in the Islamic text, prays for the future of her child. She asks that her unborn daughter will have a close relationship with God, and her final prayer hints at the special status of her future grandson Jesus. This tradition resembles the Christian noncanonical text from the late second century known as the Proto-Gospel of James, in which Mary's mother dedicates the daughter in her womb to God's service in the Jerusalem temple.

THE ANNOUNCEMENT OF JOHN'S BIRTH

The next part of the story describes the realization of that promise.

[37]Her Lord graciously accepted her. He caused her to grow up well, and He gave her into the care of Zachariah. Every time Zachariah came to see her in the chamber, he found her with provisions. He said, "Oh Mary, where did you get this?" She answered, "It is from God. Truly, God provides without measure for whomever He wishes." [38]Then and there, Zachariah called upon his Lord saying, "My Lord, grant me good offspring from Yourself. Truly, You hear all prayers." [39]Then the angels called to him while he stood praying in the chamber, "God gives you the good news of John, who will confirm a word from God. He will be noble, chaste, and a prophet from among the righteous." [40]He said, "Oh Lord, how is it that I might have a son when I am old

and my wife is barren?" He [an angel] said, "Thus it is. God does what He wills." [41]He said, "My Lord, give me a sign." He said, "Your sign is that you will not be able to speak to a person for three days except by gesture. Remember your Lord much, and praise him in the evening and in the morning." (Q 3:37–41)

Zachariah serves as Mary's caretaker in a location identified with a term (*miḥrāb*) that is translated "chamber" but can also describe a building of importance and here likely refers to the temple.[3] She has been dedicated to God as her mother promised, and the deity now preempts her human custodian by providing Mary with food and other sustenance before Zachariah can do so. The roles of the two are reversed, as Zachariah ends up relying on Mary to get what he needs. When she tells him about the source of her miraculous provisions and that God has the power to give anything, Zachariah immediately asks for a child (v. 38). God's provisions therefore serve a double purpose: they symbolize the divine protection Mary receives, and they are a springboard to Zachariah's belief and trust in God.

The description of the announcement of John's birth resembles what takes place in Luke 1:5–25: an angelic messenger responds to Zachariah's prayer to inform him that he will have a son, and then goes on to say something about what kind of man the child will become. In both texts Zachariah reacts to this news by saying that he and his wife are too old to have children, and in each one the sign that verifies the message is Zachariah's temporary muteness. Among the most notable differences between the two accounts are Mary's absence from the scene in Luke, and the Qur'an's reference to John's status as a prophet in keeping with his role in Islam (v. 39). Here, too, the story parallels the Proto-Gospel of James because Zachariah functions as Mary's caretaker in both texts.

THE ANNOUNCEMENT OF JESUS'S BIRTH

With Zachariah having received the news of John's birth, it now becomes Mary's story.

[42]The angels said, "Oh Mary, God has truly chosen you and purified you. He has chosen you above all women. [43]Oh Mary, be devout to your Lord, prostrate yourself, and be among those who bow down." [44]This is part of the hidden news that We[4] reveal to you. You were not with them when they cast lots to see which of them should take care of Mary, nor were you with them when they disputed among themselves. [45]The angels said, "Oh Mary, God gives you the good news of a word from Him. His name will be the Messiah Jesus, son of Mary, who will be eminent in this world and the next, and will be one of those brought near to God. [46]He will speak to people from the cradle and in his later years, and he will be one of the righteous ones." [47]She said, "My Lord, how can I have a child when no man has touched me?" The angels said, "Thus it is—God creates what He wills. If he decrees something, He only needs to say, 'Be!' and it is." (Q 3:42–47)

The angels' opening words to Mary highlight her purity by employing an Arabic verb that means "to make pure," surrounded by the double use of another verb that is here translated "to choose" but comes from a root that means "to be pure." The command that Mary should then prostrate herself in worship and bow down in prayer (v. 43) describes two actions central to Muslim ritual and so points to the Islamization of the tradition. The addressee of the revelation in verse 44 is grammatically masculine singular, and Muslim commentators have usually considered it to be directed at the prophet of Islam. While this is not impossible, it could also be addressed to Zachariah as he is reminded of something that happened in the past. Regardless of its intended addressee, the verse provides yet another connection with the Proto-Gospel of James. That text (8:3—9:12) describes a contest among the local eligible men to determine who would marry Mary and take care of her, and this Qur'an verse recounts a similar event.

In verses 45–46 the angels speak to Mary about Jesus, using a number of titles to describe him. Titles like *word* and *Messiah* have particular significance within Christianity. The Gospel of John refers to Jesus as the "word" as a way of conveying his divinity (see John 1:1–18). The title *Messiah*, discussed in the introduction, links Jesus to King David and the savior whom Jews anticipated God would send. These meanings ought not to be read into or assumed present in the Islamic text. In Luke's story of the annunciation, the angel Gabriel delivers the message to Mary, and he also refers to various roles and titles Jesus will have: "He will be great, and will be called the Son of the Most High, and the Lord God will give to him the throne of his ancestor David. He will reign over the house of Jacob forever, and of his kingdom there will be no end....Therefore the child to be born will be holy; he will be called Son of God" (Luke 1:32–33, 35).[5] This description of Jesus, particularly the references to him as the Son of the Most High and the Son of God, runs contrary to the Islamic understanding of his role, as discussed more fully later in this chapter.

As Mary does in Luke (1:34), the qur'anic Mary objects to the angelic message by stating that she has not had sexual relations (v. 47a). The Islamic text therefore agrees with the account in Luke (and Matthew) that Jesus was virginally conceived. It does not, however, consider this to be a sign of Jesus's divinity: the angels go on to tell Mary that such a miraculous pregnancy is God's doing but say nothing about the one who is brought into existence by the divine will (v. 47b). Unlike in the New Testament accounts of Jesus's conception and birth, Joseph plays no role in the Qur'an's accounts.[6] His absence, as well as Zachariah's relative ineffectiveness in serving as Mary's caretaker, highlight Mary's isolation and complete dependence on God, both of which are elaborated in the passage that we take up next.

The Announcement and Birth of Jesus

The other Qur'an passage that describes the annunciation of Jesus's birth to Mary does not mention Zachariah or John, and it features a single messenger from God instead of a group of angels. It is followed by a passage that contains the Qur'an's only account of Jesus's birth. The following discussion treats the text in two parts.

THE ANNUNCIATION

¹⁶Remember Mary in the book. When she withdrew from her family to a place in the east ¹⁷and took cover from them, We sent to her Our spirit that appeared to her in the form of a normal person. ¹⁸She said, "I take refuge in the merciful one from you if you fear Him." ¹⁹He said, "I am only a Messenger from your Lord, to give you a righteous son." ²⁰She said, "How can I have a son when no man has touched me and I have not been unchaste?" ²¹He said, "Thus it is. Your Lord said, 'It is easy for Me. We will make him a sign for people and a mercy from Us.' It is an accomplished fact." (Q 19:16–21)

The story opens with Mary heading east in an unspecified location, all alone and far from home. She soon encounters someone identified both as God's spirit and as a messenger who appears "in the form of a normal person" (vv. 17–19). This double description is comparable to the Genesis story in which God appears to Abraham and Sarah in the form of three men to announce to them that Sarah will bear Isaac (Gen 18:1–15). Here, although the messenger's normal appearance and his comment that he will give her a son could suggest the pregnancy will come about in the usual way, his identification as God's spirit makes clear that something extraordinary is occurring. There has been universal agreement among Muslim commentators that Mary conceived Jesus miraculously, and so they have not proposed that she and the messenger engaged in sexual relations.

Scholars have suggested various interpretations for how Mary became pregnant, with many of them centering on the messenger's designation as God's spirit. The Arabic word for "spirit" (*rūḥ*) can also mean "breath," and this has sometimes been cited as the means by which Mary was impregnated. Some have proposed that the messenger breathed into Mary's mouth, sleeve, or pocket in order that she might conceive. One interpretation suggests that after she took off her clothes to bathe, the messenger breathed into them, and when she put them back on, she became pregnant. Another text in the Qur'an describes her as "Mary, the daughter of 'Imran, who guarded her chastity, so We breathed into her Our

17

spirit" (66:12). Yet the verse describes something more graphic than what this translation implies. The Arabic word translated "chastity" (*farj*) can refer to an opening, and it is sometimes used as a euphemism for the female genitals. In addition, the prepositional phrase rendered "into her" is actually "into it" in Arabic, and the grammatical antecedent to "it" is *farj*. The verse therefore understands Jesus's conception to be the result of God (or God's messenger) breathing into Mary's genitals.[7]

As in the Qur'an's other annunciation scene, the present text highlights Mary's trust and faith in God. Once again, Joseph is not mentioned, and in this version she does not even have Zachariah to serve as a guardian. In both passages, when she objects she is told that God can do anything, and so she must accept what she has been told. A key difference becomes apparent when we compare these texts with the biblical account. In Luke, Mary receives a sign that what the angel has said will come to pass when she visits her relative, Zachariah's wife Elizabeth, and learns that the older woman is also expecting a child (Luke 1:36, 39–56). Mary receives no such sign in the Qur'an and must accept on her own the truth of the messenger's words with no external verification. In this way, the Qur'an consistently presents her as the ideal Muslim who must submit fully to the divine will. The biblical Mary speaks perhaps her most famous statement in response to Gabriel's message: "Here am I, the servant of the Lord; let it be with me according to your word" (Luke 1:38). Although she does not utter those words in the Qur'an, they align perfectly with the way the Islamic text presents her.

THE BIRTH

[22]She conceived him and withdrew with him to a distant place. [23]The birth pangs led her to the trunk of a palm tree where she cried, "Oh, if only I had died before this and had been forgotten, unremembered!" [24]Then [a voice] called out to her from below her, "Do not grieve! Your Lord has placed a stream beneath you. [25]Shake the trunk of the palm tree and it will drop fresh ripe dates upon you. [26]Eat, drink, and be consoled. If you should see another person, say, 'I have vowed a fast to the merciful

one and will not speak to anyone today'." ²⁷She carried him [Jesus] to her people, who said, "Oh Mary, you have done something strange! ²⁸Oh sister of Aaron, your father was not wicked nor was your mother unchaste." ²⁹She pointed at him, and they said, "How can we talk to a child in the cradle?" (Q 19:22–29)

Jesus's birth story opens with Mary isolating herself yet further (v. 22). Once again, her destination is not identified, but the story suggests a desolate area because she is alone, hungry, thirsty, and wishes she were dead. Her words in verse 23 are full of misery and likely due to her physical pain or mental distress. There is an ironic dimension to her desire to be forgotten because that was certainly not her fate, and as the only woman mentioned by name in the Qur'an she has been widely recognized and celebrated among Muslims.

The most unusual aspect of the passage is the voice that speaks to Mary in her distress and urges her to not give in to her despair. Who speaks these words? They come from beneath her, and so the most logical answer to that question is that the newborn Jesus is speaking to his mother soon after she has given birth to him. That is how most Muslim commentators interpret the scene, and they consider his ability to speak as an infant to be the first of the miracles Jesus performed. The palm tree tradition could be related to an apocryphal Christian writing known as the Infancy Gospel of Pseudo-Matthew that might have been written as early as the sixth century and relates traditions about the trip that Joseph, Mary, and Jesus took to Egypt to escape Herod's oppression (see Matt 2:13–23). In chapter 20 of that work a palm tree obeys Jesus's orders to bow down and to provide sustenance to Mary from its fruit, and then opens up its roots to quench the family's thirst.

The passage concludes with Mary returning home and being chastised for having a child out of wedlock (vv. 27–29). That she is referred to as "sister of Aaron" may reflect the biblical tradition that describes her relative Elizabeth as a descendant of Aaron (Luke 1:5), or it may reflect the fact that Aaron and Moses had a sister whose name, Miriam, is a variant of Mary (*maryam* in Arabic). As noted above, Mary's father in the Qur'an has the same name as Moses's father in Jewish tradition, and this could reflect confusion or a conflation of the two figures. Muslim scholars have not endorsed the possibility of such confusion, suggesting that either Mary did have a brother named Aaron, or she was Aaron's (and Moses's) sister in a metaphorical or symbolic way.

The rejection Mary experiences when she returns to "her people" raises the question of whether or not she might be viewed as a prophet in the Qur'an. The reference to "her people" (v. 27) supports this interpretation since this is how the Qur'an consistently describes a prophet's community. The identification of Jesus as God's word is intriguing in this regard because bringing God's word is an essential aspect of a prophet's mission. Moreover, in a chapter that has the title "The Prophets," the Qur'an mentions Mary among a total of eighteen individuals referred to by name (21:91), but she is the only one of them not explicitly recognized as a prophet. Should she be included among their ranks? Very few Muslim commentators have entertained that possibility, and they have often appealed to other passages in the Qur'an that allegedly limit the prophetic role to males (Q 12:109; 16:43). Nevertheless, the terms *prophet* and *male* are not found in those two verses. Centuries of Muslim tradition and scholarship are opposed to the idea of Mary as a prophet, but certain aspects of her role in the Qur'an might suggest otherwise.

Jesus in the Qur'an

The Qur'an mentions the name of Jesus twenty-five times, usually accompanied by a title or other designation. The two most common titles used in connection with him are *son of Mary* and *Messiah*. The former is most likely a way of stressing his humanity, but the Qur'an never explains the word *Messiah* and so it is difficult to know what its meaning there might be. No other person in the Islamic text is called a Messiah, and in reference to Jesus the term may simply represent a dignified title for him borrowed from Christian usage. The following passage neatly summarizes the Islamic understanding of Jesus:

> People of the Book, do not exceed the bounds of your religion, and speak only the truth about God. The Messiah

> Jesus, son of Mary, was God's messenger and His word
> He sent to Mary, and a spirit from Him. So believe in
> God and His messengers and do not say "Three." Desist
> and it will be better for you, for truly God is one God. It
> is beyond Him to have a son. All that is in the heavens
> and on the earth belongs to Him. God is the only protec-
> tor. (Q 4:171)

This verse identifies Jesus with several titles—*Messiah, son of Mary, messenger, God's word,* and *God's spirit*. No other figure in the Qur'an is described in so many different ways, indicating the special status Jesus has in Islam. Yet it omits New Testament titles that convey divine status, such as *Lord*. As noted above, Christians ought not to read their own understanding of titles like God's word and Messiah into the Qur'an. The latter part of the verse goes on to state that Jesus's roles as word and spirit do not mean he is divine.

In this passage and elsewhere, the Qur'an challenges and critiques two beliefs that are central to Christianity: the incarnation, which affirms that in Jesus God became a human being; and the Trinity, the idea that God is three persons in one. The passage grants Jesus another lofty title by referring to him as a messenger: like Moses before him and Muhammad after him, Jesus received from God a message for his people in the form of a book. This book is identified in the Qur'an as the Injil (*injīl*), an Arabicized form of the Greek word for "gospel" (*euangelion*). Jesus's book confirmed and did not nullify the earlier scriptures (Q 5:46), but according to Islam it was rendered obsolete by the Qur'an because Jesus's followers did not accurately preserve the contents of the Injil, and this made necessary the coming of Muhammad and his book. Christian tradition refers to the teaching of Jesus as the gospel, but it does not attribute a book to him.

The Qur'an also teaches that Jesus would never object to being God's servant, and this is illustrated in chapter 19 after Mary's people complain that it would be impossible for them to converse with an infant. In the very next verse the baby Jesus does speak, and he leaves no doubt as to his relationship with God.

> ³⁰He [Jesus] said, "I am a servant of God. He has given me the book and has made me a prophet. ³¹He has made me blessed wherever I may be, and He has commanded me to observe prayer and almsgiving for as long as I live. ³²He has made me obedient to my mother, and has not made me proud or miserable. ³³Peace upon me the day I was born, the day I will die and the day I will be raised to life." (Q 19:30–33)

Jesus's very first words as a newborn put him in a subservient relationship with God (v. 30). Further Islamization of the figure of Jesus appears in his statement that God has ordered him to engage in prayer and almsgiving (v. 31), two practices that are central to the Muslim faith.

In another passage, Jesus explains his role and relationship with God, but it can be difficult for Christians to read because it can be read in a way that has him contradict the doctrines of the incarnation and the Trinity.

> ⁷²They disbelieve who say, "God is the Messiah, son of Mary." The Messiah said, "Oh children of Israel, worship God, my Lord and your Lord." Whoever associates something with God, paradise has been denied to that person and the fire will be their abode. There will be no helpers for the evildoers. ⁷³They disbelieve who say, "God is the third of three." There is no god but the one God. If they do not desist from what they say, a painful punishment will come upon those who disbelieve. (Q 5:72–73)

On the one hand, although this translation has Jesus's words conclude, "and your Lord," there is no grammatical reason why his comments cannot extend to the end of the passage—there are no quotation marks in Arabic. If we read the text that way, then Jesus is stating that Christians will be punished for believing that he is divine, and the text goes on to say that if they turn to God and repent they will be forgiven; Christians would have to reject core beliefs of their religion.⁸ On the other hand, compelling factors support the present translation in not extending Jesus's words further: Jesus does not issue the threat of hellfire anywhere else in the Qur'an, and similar references to association, paradise, and fire are found throughout the Qur'an in passages that do not quote people from the past. In any case, the passage clearly contradicts these two key Christian beliefs.

Christians must not jump to the wrong conclusion about why the Qur'an rejects key elements of their faith. Such rejection does not imply animosity or disrespect for Christianity, but simply reflects the way Islam understands monotheism, which is so central to its system of belief. Muslims believe that God is one, and anything that violates the divine unity (*tawḥīd*) is considered an example of the sin of the association (*shirk*) of something in the created world with the uncreated nature of God. The Qur'an teaches that belief in the divinity of Jesus is an example of such an association and therefore a violation of God's oneness.

At the same time, the manner in which the Qur'an construes Christian belief in the Trinity is problematic from a Christian perspective. For example, verse 73 of the passage cited above characterizes Christianity as believing in three gods. Yet Christians maintain that belief in the three persons of the Trinity does not violate God's unity. In the history of Christianity it took centuries for Christians themselves to develop and agree upon this doctrine.[9] It is therefore incumbent upon Muslims not simply to rely on Qur'an passages like this one, but to learn how Christianity understands God in relationship to Jesus.

The Qur'an mentions some of Jesus's miraculous works, although it does not describe them in the detail that New Testament texts do. After the angels tell Mary about her pregnancy, they go on to quote Jesus's description of deeds he will perform.

> He [God] will make him [Jesus] a messenger to the children of Israel. [Jesus will say,] "I have come to you with a sign from your Lord. I will make a bird-shaped form for you out of clay, and then breathe into it and, by God's leave, it will become a real bird. I will heal the blind and the leprous, and I will bring the dead back to life by God's leave." (3:49)

While the canonical Gospels do not recount a miracle involving a clay bird, a similar story is found in the extracanonical Infancy

Gospel of Thomas from the second century, and its presence in the Qur'an suggests the early Muslim community was familiar with this tradition. The references here and elsewhere to Jesus performing these works of wonder "by God's leave" is a subtle reminder of Jesus's subordination to and dependence upon the deity, and therefore an example of the Islamization of traditions about him.

In Islam Jesus's death does not have the salvific significance it has in Christianity. The Qur'an refers to it in a few passages but does not describe how it occurred. The most important text that treats Jesus's death is in chapter 4 (vv. 153–59), which can be read in a way that suggests he did not actually die on the cross. A portion of verse 157 reads, "They [the Jewish people] did not kill him nor did they crucify him, but it was made to appear so to them." The phrase "it was made to appear so to them" can also be translated "he was made to appear so to them," and this has led many commentators to claim that someone else was made to look like Jesus and died in his place. If Jesus did not die on the cross, the Christian belief that he was resurrected after his crucifixion is called into question. Therefore, this interpretation of the Jesus tradition in the Qur'an is an indirect way of denying the foundational event that led to Christian belief in the divinity of Jesus.

A final passage related to Jesus shows how the Qur'an offers its own interpretation of him: "Jesus, son of Mary, said, 'Children of Israel, I am God's messenger to you, attesting to the truth already in the Torah and announcing the good news of a messenger who will come after me whose name will be Ahmad'" (Q 61:6). Ahmad is an alternative form of the name Muhammad, and so in this verse Jesus predicts the coming of the messenger of Islam. As is the case with other biblical figures, Jesus is presented here in a way that is meant to validate Muhammad's role as a prophet.

New Testament Interpretations of Mary and Jesus

One could characterize the entire New Testament as a collection of diverse interpretations of Jesus. Even the ways in which the

Gospels present Mary, his mother, communicate something about her son. As already discussed, these early Christian texts present Jesus as a man who taught a message about God, died, was raised from the dead, and continues to be present to believers through faith. At the core of Christian faith is the paradoxical belief that Jesus fulfilled the hopes of Jews for a Messiah/Christ, a successor to King David who would save them from oppression, but that he accomplished this by dying and being raised from the dead; while the saving act he accomplished was not a military or explicitly political one, it was no less real. Those texts attest to the powerful, mysterious experience of encountering the risen Jesus; the meaning of that experience for believers could not be captured completely in any single description or explanation, of either events or teachings. Their experience led believers to refer to Jesus using terms for God found in the Jewish scriptures, for example *Lord* and the phrase *I am*. Believers accepted the New Testament texts as authoritative because they found that their experience of faith in Jesus resonated with the range of stories, images, sayings, and teachings contained in them.

One characteristic that made the texts compelling was the creative manner in which they addressed the concrete struggles that believers faced as they tried to persevere in the path of faith. The earliest believers struggled between feeling encouraged and energized by their prayerful experience of the risen Christ, and feeling discouraged, afraid, and unconvinced of their belief in him. Many New Testament interpretations of Jesus speak to such struggles by attesting to the possibility of encountering him even in the midst of doubts, anxieties, and suffering. This ability to speak to people's concrete struggles in creative ways has been a significant factor in how these texts have proven compelling across generations and cultures for believers, most of whom struggle with faith at some point.

Recognizing that a comprehensive treatment of New Testament interpretations of Jesus and Mary lies beyond the scope of this book, the following brief discussion seeks to provide some orientation to the topic. It first offers a comparison of the ways in which the canonical Gospels interpret Jesus, employing examples from the resurrection narratives. Then, in dialogue with the preceding discussion of the Qur'an, it briefly discusses the interpretation of Mary in Luke 1—2, and New Testament perspectives related to Christian belief in the incarnation and the Trinity.

THE GOSPELS INTERPRET JESUS

The four Gospels were written for believers decades after the death of Jesus. Recognizing this fact helps to understand why their descriptions of events prior to his death, as well as events related to his resurrection, all interpret Jesus in ways that communicate about the risen Jesus. The Gospels address believers' desire to encounter him and to better live in response to such encounters. From the earliest generations, their texts were read aloud during communal worship, known as liturgy, and especially during Eucharist, the central Christian liturgy that remembers Jesus's final meal with his disciples before his death. In such prayerful contexts, their texts shaped the imaginations of believers who sought to recognize Jesus's presence in their ordinary lives. For example, scholars have long recognized that the various stories about Jesus feeding multitudes—aside from the question of the degree to which the stories reflect historical events—helped Christians to reflect on their own experience of encountering him in the liturgical meal of Eucharist.[10] As do other New Testament texts, all four Gospels interpret Jesus as both consoling and challenging believers. They emphasize the ways in which an experience of the risen Christ not only offers people peace and reconciliation with God, but also moves them to witness about Christ to others, and to do so not merely in words but also by selfless acts of service, and especially by caring for the needy and the vulnerable.

The first resurrection account in all four Gospels describes how the disciples saw the empty tomb of Jesus before any of them encountered the risen Jesus (Matt 28:1–10; Mark 16:1–9; Luke 24:1–12; John 20:1–10). In all four versions of this scene Jesus has died, the tomb is open, and his body is gone. The scene is rich with possible meaning, including how encountering the risen Jesus requires faith and occurs as one faces and lets go of the loss of what was familiar or expected. Thus, the scene echoes the conviction attested in many New Testament texts that believers can experience the consoling presence of the risen Jesus, especially in the midst of suffering and loss, but that such an experience is not obvious or automatic; it occurs through faith. The Synoptic (Matthew, Mark, and Luke) versions of the empty tomb scene describe how, upon receiving the news of the resurrection from one or two angelic figures, the women experienced powerful feelings, including amazement and fear. Such descriptions would have resonated with early Christians who encountered the risen Jesus in unexpected ways and amid their own fears.

Let us consider a couple ways in which the descriptions of the scene in Mark and John interpret Jesus differently. The version in Mark describes the women's fear by saying that despite the angel's instruction to tell the news to the disciples, they were trembling, amazed, and did not tell anyone because they were afraid (Mark 16:8). This detail resonates with the way that this Gospel highlights that believing in Jesus requires willingness to follow Jesus, even if doing so entails suffering and death. The version in John emphasizes the love that Mary Magdalene has for Jesus and her consequent sadness at not being able to care properly for his dead body. This story would have helped early Christians to imagine opening the affective dimension of themselves to encountering the risen Jesus. The scene in John continues as Jesus appears to Mary Magdalene, who initially thinks he is a gardener and only recognizes him after "turning," a term that signifies change of heart and conversion, in response to his calling her by name (John 20:11–17). This tender, loving encounter echoes John's emphasis on Jesus as loving those who believe in him, and through his love for them enabling them to let go of their own attachments and expectations, and to believe in him and serve others in loving and selfless ways.

INTERPRETATION OF MARY IN LUKE 1—2

While identifying Jesus as Savior, Christ/Messiah, Lord, and Son of God (1:35; 2:11), Luke invites readers to identify both with Mary's willingness to receive God's activity in herself, and with her participation in God's activity through interacting with others. In Luke, Mary goes to visit her cousin Elizabeth for support (1:39–56), and she receives a group of strangers, shepherds, immediately after giving birth (2:16). In bringing Mary and Elizabeth together, and in bringing shepherds to the scene of Jesus's birth, Luke develops an image that runs throughout the Gospel and links these scenes to the disciples' encounter with the risen Jesus. This image is one of joy emanating from encounters among people who experience what God is doing in Jesus and share that experience. Along with its companion volume, Acts of the Apostles, Luke portrays Jesus's birth, ministry, death, and resurrection, as well as the ongoing presence of the Holy Spirit among believers—all of these—as part of the same activity of God. Luke invites the reader to participate in this activity, as did Mary.

In Luke and Acts, a key dynamic effect of God's activity among believers is joy.[11] When greeting Mary, Elizabeth declares, "For as soon as I heard the sound of your greeting, the child in my womb leaped for joy" (Luke 1:44). In announcing Jesus's birth to shepherds, the angel of the Lord declares, "Do not be afraid; for see—I am bringing you good news of great joy for all the people" (Luke 2:10). It is this declaration that prompts them to go in haste to see Mary, Joseph, and the child, and after the encounter, they share the news so that all who hear them are amazed (Luke 2:15–18). When two of Jesus's disciples are leaving Jerusalem with heavy hearts after his death, they do not recognize that Jesus is the stranger walking with them until he breaks bread with them (Luke 24:13–32). As soon as they recognize him, he vanishes from their sight, they become aware that their hearts had been burning in them while he was with them, and they return immediately to the disciples in Jerusalem to report what had happened—their joy is obvious (Luke 24:31–35). Then, the gathered disciples respond with joy both when the risen Jesus appears to them and after he withdraws from them (Luke 24:41, 52). As do other New Testament texts (e.g., Matt 18:20), Luke recognizes that encountering God's activity in the risen Christ and experiencing its joy can depend on people engaging with each other in a context of faith. Seen in this light, Mary in Luke 1—2 serves as a model for engaging others with openness in faith to God's activity in Christ.

THE PRACTICAL ASPECT OF PORTRAYING JESUS'S DIVINITY

The early believers' experience of the risen Jesus through faith was beyond words, and yet words remained an important medium through which to communicate about that experience. This is perhaps the best starting point from which to consider New Testament portrayals of Jesus in relationship to what centuries later became the clearly articulated Christian beliefs about the incarnation and the Trinity contained in the Nicene Creed. On the one hand, if the early Christians had not claimed to experience the risen Jesus, it is difficult to imagine that their traditions of portraying him as divine would have gained any enduring acceptance. On the other hand, the various titles, images, stories, and teachings in the New Testament that convey Jesus's divinity functioned primarily in a practical rather than theoretical manner. They facilitated both prayerful experience of encountering the risen Jesus and reflective understanding of what that experience meant on various levels, including continuity with Jewish tradition and implications for ethical issues. Thus, it is easy to understand how Muslims and Jews, who profess belief in one God as do Christians but do not share the Christian claim to experience the risen Jesus through faith, would object to claims about Jesus that equate him with God. The following example illustrates the practical function of New Testament interpretations of Jesus's divinity for believers.

The Gospel of Mark begins by identifying Jesus as the Son of God (1:1), and in Mark's accounts of Jesus's baptism and the transfiguration, a voice from heaven identifies him as "my Son, the Beloved" (1:11; 9:7). However, throughout this Gospel Jesus does not allow either his disciples or the demons that he casts out of people to identify him as the Messiah or the Son of God (e.g., 1:32–34; 8:29–30). After he has died on the cross, Mark portrays a Roman centurion (who may have presided over the execution) declaring of Jesus, "Truly this man was God's Son!" (15:39). From early Christianity to the present, Christians can be tempted to focus on believing in Jesus's divinity primarily out of an expectation that he might give them something as a result, such as a miraculous solution to problems or an enhanced personal status (e.g., Mark 10:35–45). One practical result of presenting Jesus's divinity as Mark does is to invite readers to anticipate the mysterious transformation that occurs only through following Jesus to the cross: seeking the risen Jesus in the midst of the struggle, suffering, and even death that following him in daily living might entail. Mark's presentation of the parable of the sower invites readers to reflect

29

on precisely the mysterious character of that transformation (4:1–20). Of that parable Jesus explains, "To you has been given the secret [mystery] of the kingdom of God, but for those outside, everything comes in parables" (Mark 4:11). In that parable, the seed sown on good soil yields up to one hundredfold, and Jesus's explanation clarifies how such an amazing abundance captures the mystery of the transformation that those who accept Jesus's invitation to the cross will experience.

Focus for Comparison

Jesus has undergone a more dramatic and radical interpretation than any other biblical figure in the Qur'an, which shows familiarity with some of the core Christian beliefs about Jesus, but it interprets him to be a human being and nothing more. The Muslim text could even be seen to have Jesus himself disavow claims that he is divine. In the Qur'an, the Christian Son of God and Savior has been replaced by the Muslim prophet Jesus, Son of Mary. But that is only part of the story. Jesus has also been interpreted by members of the community that express faith in him as the Son of God. The differences in what the two sets of scriptures say about Jesus are best understood in light of the different purposes for which they were written. For Muslims, the Qur'an invites readers to submit completely to the merciful God, whose words it preserves perfectly, as recorded by the great Prophet Muhammad. Christians wrote the New Testament—with its range of stories, images, and teachings—to help readers relate to God by encountering the risen Jesus in affectively charged ways even when suffering, and from that encounter to live in service of God and others, especially the oppressed. The portrayals of Jesus that emerge in the New Testament and the Qur'an, like those of every other figure treated in this book, are composites that have been shaped by things both new and old.

Questions to Consider

1. In what way(s) might it be considered problematic that the Qur'an denies key elements of Christian belief about Jesus?

2. Might the Qur'an's references to Jesus as a "word" and "spirit" be helpful to Christian/Muslim relations? If so, how?

3. Which is more apparent in how Mary is presented in the Qur'an and the Bible, similarities or differences?

4. How might the connections between the Qur'an and noncanonical Christian writings like the Proto-Gospel of James and the Infancy Gospel of Thomas be explained?

5. What are we to make of the seeming connection the Qur'an makes between Moses and Mary through her father's name and her title *sister of Aaron*?

6. What are the most important things that Christians and Muslims can agree on regarding Jesus?

7. In what way(s) might Jesus be ultimately a help or a hindrance to relations between Muslims and Christians?

CHAPTER 2

Adam and Eve

The Qur'an agrees with the Bible that the first human being was Adam, but it does not identify his female partner by name. Other early Islamic sources call her Eve, but she remains unnamed in the Qur'an. The only woman whose name is mentioned in Islamic scripture is Mary, the mother of Jesus. The idea that there was a first couple to whom all other people can trace their origin is found in Qur'an 4:1a, where both members are anonymous: "Oh people, be mindful of your Lord, who created you from a single soul, and created from it its mate. From them spread out many men and women." According to this verse, Eve was somehow formed from Adam, but the Qur'an does not describe exactly how her creation came about (cf. Q 39:6). The Qur'an contains several different accounts of the creation of humanity, and two of them will be discussed here. But first another character who plays an important role in those passages but is not mentioned in the Bible's account of human creation must be considered.

Iblis, the Fallen Angel

Iblis is a figure to whom the Qur'an refers eleven times. While there is some debate about the origin of his name, it is most likely an Arabicized version of the Greek word *diabolos*, from which the English "devil" is derived. He is most frequently mentioned in stories about Adam's creation that explain how Iblis refused God's order to bow down to the first human being (Q 2:34–39; 7:10–18;

15:28–48; 17:61–65; 18:50; 20:115–23; 38:67–84). That act of rebellion led to his expulsion from paradise, but not before he vowed to be humanity's enemy. When God questions him about his refusal to comply with his command, Iblis answers in a prideful way that indicates he considers himself to be superior to Adam. In some versions of the story, God responds favorably to Iblis's appeal to the deity for mercy.

There is an aura of mystery about Iblis's precise identity in the Qur'an because he is also associated with other figures mentioned in the creation story. He is among the angels because when God commands the angels to bow down before Adam, Iblis is singled out as the only one who refuses to comply with that order (Q 2:34; 7:11; 15:30–31; 17:61; 18:50; 38:73–74). Yet a bit later in the story he appears to change into Satan, who tricks Adam and Eve into eating the fruit of the tree from which God has prohibited them to eat (Q 2:34–36; 7:11–20; 20:115–20). In addition, one passage describes Iblis as one of the jinn (*jinn*), a group of supernatural beings that have the capacity to interact with humans in ways both helpful and harmful.[1] That verse also states that Iblis has offspring, something angels are incapable of according to Islamic tradition (Q 18:50). In support of his being one of the jinn is Iblis's claim that he was created from fire, from which the Qur'an says the jinn were made (Q 55:15). Perhaps the accounts of the garden story in the Qur'an portray Iblis as undergoing a transformation: he was originally created as an angel, but when he disobeyed God and refused to bow down to Adam, he became one of the jinn. Prior to that refusal he was known as Iblis, but after it he was identified as Satan.

There is no exact equivalent to Iblis in the Bible, but some Jewish texts preserve a tradition similar to the description of him in these qur'anic passages. A set of writings known as the Life of Adam and Eve (also called Apocalypse of Moses) present a scene in which Satan refuses God's command to bow down to Adam and is expelled from paradise. These texts, preserved in Greek and Latin, were written between the third and fifth centuries CE, although they likely trace their roots to the first century CE. The similarities between the two suggest that the Jewish tradition was known in Arabia during Muhammad's lifetime.

A Garden Story

A description of Iblis's disobedience precedes the story of Adam and Eve in the garden as told in Qur'an 7:10–25, which includes the following elements that are commonly found in the Qur'an's other accounts of the events (Q 2:28–39; 15:19–48; 20:115–23):

1. God places the couple in a garden to live.
2. God forbids them to eat from a particular tree.
3. Satan persuades them to eat from the tree.
4. The couple realizes they are naked and cover themselves.
5. The couple has a conversation with God in which they admit their mistake.
6. The couple is expelled from the garden.

[10]We have set you firmly in the earth and provided you with a livelihood, but you give little thanks. [11]We created you and then gave you shape. Then We said to the angels, "Prostrate yourselves before Adam," and they all did so except Iblis, who was not among those who prostrated. [12]God asked, "What prevented you from prostrating when I ordered you?" He replied, "You created me of fire, but you created him of clay." [13]God said, "Go down from here! You are not to be proud here. Leave! You are among those despised!" [14]Iblis said, "Grant to me a delay until the day they are raised up." [15]God said, "You are among those who are reprieved." [16]Iblis then said, "Because You have caused me to err, I will surely lie in wait for them on Your straight path. [17]Then I will come upon them from the front and from behind, upon their right side and their left side. Then You will not find the majority of them thankful." [18]God said, "Be gone, banished and driven away! As for those that follow you, I will surely fill Hell with all of you. Oh Adam, you and your wife live in the garden, and eat from where you wish; but do not approach this tree, or

you will be among those who do wrong." [20]But Satan whispered to them so that he might reveal to them what was hidden from them of their shame. He said, "Your Lord has forbidden for you to approach this tree only to prevent you from becoming angels or immortals." [21]Then he swore to them, "I am truly among those who give honest advice to you." [22]Thus did he guide them by deceit. When they had tasted of the tree their nakedness became apparent to them, and they began to cover themselves with the leaves of the garden. Their Lord called out to them, "Did I not forbid you to approach the tree, and did I not warn you that Satan is a clear enemy to you?" [23]They replied, "Our Lord, we have harmed ourselves. If You do not forgive us and have mercy on us, we shall surely be among the lost." [24]He said, "Go! Some of you will be enemies of each other. For a while, the earth will provide you a dwelling and life's necessities. [25]There you shall live and there you shall die, and from there you shall be brought out." (Q 7:10–25)

COMPARISON WITH THE BIBLICAL NARRATIVE

Once Iblis leaves the scene, there is much in the Qur'an passage that aligns with the events described in Genesis 2—3. This list identifies the most obvious points of contact between the two accounts.

1. Location in a garden (Q 7:19; Gen 2:8, 15)
2. Human creation from clay (Q 7:12; Gen 2:7)
3. Admonition to not eat from the tree (Q 7:19; Gen 2:16–17)
4. A deceitful agent who acts as the couple's confidante (Q 7:20–21; Gen 3:1)
5. An agent who claims to know God's intent (Q 7:20–21; Gen 3:4)
6. Covering of nakedness (Q 7:22; Gen 3:7, 21)

7. A conversation between God and the couple
   (Q 7:22–23; Gen 3:9–19)
8. Expulsion from the garden (Q 7:24; Gen 3:24)

The Qur'an story follows closely the plot of the biblical one, but they are not identical. When parallel traditions exist in the Bible and the Qur'an, various differences can usually be noted between them, with some being minor variations and others having a significant impact on the way the story unfolds and the lesson the reader takes from it. Such differences often provide clues about how the Qur'an has interpreted the biblical tradition, and paying careful attention to them allows us to see the interpretive process at work.

INTERPRETATION OF ADAM AND EVE

The Qur'an sometimes includes information lacking in its biblical parallel about why a story is being told or what will take place in it. For the reader, doing so can identify a central theme of the story or anticipate how the plot will unfold. Such a telegraphing technique can be seen at the end of the first verse of this Qur'an passage, where the reference to all God has done for humanity is followed by the comment, "but you give little thanks." That simple phrase, only three words in the original Arabic, provides the lens through which the story that is about to be told should be viewed—human beings' lack of appreciation toward their Creator. This is a story about people's inability to appreciate and be grateful for what God has given them. The Genesis creation account simply describes what happens; it does not offer a similar statement that tips off the reader as to the lesson behind the story.

The Qur'an text does not offer a detailed description of human creation, but it agrees with Genesis that Adam was created from the earth (v. 12; Gen 2:7). Similarly, both the Bible and the Qur'an describe God's act of creating humanity by using verbs in Hebrew and Arabic that can convey the idea of shaping or sculpting, thereby presenting the deity's actions in artistic terms (v. 11; Gen 2:7). Elsewhere, the Islamic text describes the deity's creation of the first human being in a similarly physical way: "God said, 'Oh Iblis, why do you not bow down to the human being I have made with My own hands? Are you too proud and mighty?'" (Q 38:75).

The intimate manner in which God brought about Adam's existence is also underscored in the description of how the divine breath animated the first human, a mode of creation that is also found in Genesis: "When I have fashioned him and breathed in him of My spirit, prostrate yourselves before him" (Q 15:29; cf. 38:72; Gen 2:7).

There is no separate creation of Eve in the Qur'an passage as there is in the Bible, where God uses Adam's rib to form her (Gen 2:21–22). Her creation from Adam has sometimes been interpreted as an indication of her inferior status in relation to him, as has the description of Eve as Adam's "helper" (Gen 2:18). Neither of these interpretations stands up to scrutiny because Adam was created from the dust of the earth and is not inferior to it, and the Hebrew term that identifies Eve as Adam's helper is used elsewhere in the Bible to describe God. Nonetheless, the notion that Adam was superior to Eve and that she was the one primarily responsible for the couple's difficulties is often found in the history of interpretation of the biblical passage, and the garden story has sometimes been cited to support misogynistic and patriarchal views.

Such positions cannot be defended by this Qur'an passage, which places the couple on equal footing and presents an egalitarian picture of the relationship between Adam and Eve. There is no two-step process of creation in which he comes on the scene first, and no distinction is made between the man and the woman that suggests one of them is privileged over the other. They act jointly at each step along the way, and their teamwork is reinforced by an interesting feature of Arabic grammar. Unlike English, in which the pronoun *you* does double duty as both a singular and a plural form, Arabic has different pronouns depending on whether one person or many people are being referenced. In addition, Arabic makes use of a dual form that is employed when speaking to or about two individuals. This passage has one of the highest concentrations of the latter in the entire Qur'an; in the space of just four verses (vv. 19–22), nouns and verbs appear in the dual form a remarkable twenty-eight times. This fact suggests that both Adam and Eve were completely involved in what happened and equally responsible for the outcome. Whereas in the Bible Eve has a conversation with the serpent and eats before giving the fruit to Adam (Gen 3:1–6), in the Qur'an they listen and act in tandem, and there is only one possible answer to the question of who is culpable—both of them.

This shared culpability explains why the Qur'an lacks the finger pointing of the biblical text, where Adam attempts to blame both Eve and God after he is confronted about eating the fruit of the tree (Gen 3:11–12). Rather than play the blame game, the couple in the Islamic text remains united by acknowledging their joint offense and begging that God might show them compassion (v. 23). Those are the only words that Eve speaks in the entire Qur'an, and they are uttered in partnership with Adam. The deity then sends them from the garden to earth for a temporary period, after which they will be brought forth upon their deaths (vv. 24–25).

There is no Iblis or Satan figure in the Genesis story, where a serpent is the one who deceives the couple. This difference in the agent of deceit has a subtle effect on how the deity is viewed. The biblical text identifies the serpent as "more crafty than any other wild animal that the Lord God had made" (Gen 3:1), and the serpent exercises that divinely bestowed craftiness when it tricks Adam and Eve into eating the fruit. This raises some important questions about the deity because it suggests that in creating the serpent, God made the couple's offense possible. Is God ultimately responsible for what happened to them? Why would the deity create something that could have such an adverse effect on another part of creation? The presence of Iblis/Satan in the Qur'an story allows it to direct the reader's attention away from God and toward the fallen angel, who appears to be exercising free will in his decision to refuse to bow down to Adam and then to continue to trouble humanity. Unlike the serpent, who is simply acting in the way God created it, Iblis willfully disobeys the deity and acts on his own. In this way the Qur'an lessens the theological problem present in Genesis by placing the blame on another character who chooses to ignore the divine will rather than submit to it, as the serpent does when it acts in conformance with how it has been created. This is consistent with the qur'anic view of the deity, who always acts mercifully and is not the cause of pain or sorrow for humanity or any other part of creation.

The outcome of the story is more hopeful in the Qur'an than in the Bible. According to the Genesis account, all three of the non-divine characters are punished for their actions, as the serpent must forever crawl on its belly, the woman will experience pain when she gives birth to children, and the man will be able to work the land only after great effort and toil (Gen 3:14–19). The fracturing of the divine-human relationship is represented by the cherubim and flaming sword that are put in place to prevent reentry into the garden (Gen 3:24). The couple is also expelled in the Qur'an, but they are told that they will eventually be brought back out of the earth, hinting at the possibility of a reunion with God after they die (vv. 24–25). God's admonition in the Islamic text that they remove themselves from the garden is a type of punishment, but it is not as harsh as those in the biblical text since the deity informs them that they might be reinstated in the future.

The biblical story conveys theological perspectives through narrative detail, but the Qur'an passage provides explicit interpretation by framing its version with two sections that indicate a lesson for all people regarding what took place in the garden. The brief introduction to the story contains a number of pronouns and verbal forms in the second person plural that indicate the passage is directed to humanity at large (vv. 10–11a). Such comments directed at the Qur'an's readers or hearers are a standard feature of the text, different from the direct speech with which God addresses a character in a passage, as in verses 11–19. Similarly, after the couple is expelled from the garden, several verses are addressed to the "children of Adam," a phrase commonly used in the Qur'an to refer to all human beings: "Oh, Children of Adam, We have sent down to you clothing to cover your shame as adornment. But the clothing of piety is better. Oh, Children of Adam, do not let Satan seduce you as he sent out your parents from the garden. He stripped their clothing from them that He might show them their shame" (Q 7:26–27a). Coming immediately after the account of the first couple's encounter with Iblis/Satan, these verses universalize that story and cause readers to consider the personal implications of it for their own lives.

Another Garden Story

The Qur'an contains another version of the garden story in chapter 20 (vv. 115–23a), and like the one in chapter 7 just discussed,

it is preceded by an account of Iblis's disobedience.[2] In the following outline, the items in bold indicate those elements in chapter 20
that are not found in chapter 7.

1. **God warns Adam about Iblis.**
2. **God reminds Adam about the benefits of remaining
   in the garden.**
3. Satan persuades the couple to eat from the tree.
4. The couple realizes they are naked and cover
   themselves.
5. **God accepts Adam's repentance and guides him.**
6. The couple is expelled from the garden.

[115]Earlier, We made a covenant with Adam but he forgot. We did not find in him any resolve. [116]When We
said to the angels, "Prostrate yourselves before Adam,"
they all prostrated except Iblis, who refused. [117]We said,
"Oh Adam, this one is an enemy to you and to your
wife. Do not let him drive the two of you out of the garden and make you miserable. [118]For in it you will not be
hungry or naked, [119]you will not be thirsty or scorched
by the sun." [120]Then Satan whispered to him saying,
"Oh Adam, shall I show you the tree of immortality and
a kingdom that does not pass away?" [121]And then they
both ate from it so that their shame became apparent to
them, and they began to cover themselves with the leaves
of the garden. Thus did Adam disobey his Lord and go
astray. [122]Then his Lord chose him, returned to him with
forgiveness, and guided him. [123]God said, "Leave the garden as each other's enemy." (Q 20:115–23a)

This section about Iblis's disobedience is more abbreviated
than the one in chapter 7, and the role of Eve is reduced somewhat; while she is not mentioned specifically, Adam is referred to
by name six times. The absence of the following elements mentioned in the story in chapter 7 demonstrates that Iblis plays a
relatively minor role here: an explanation of why he refuses to
prostrate to Adam, a conversation between him and God in which

Iblis asks to be pardoned, Satan's threat to seduce God's servants, and a detailed description of Satan's deception of the couple.

The focus on Adam, along with Eve's limited role, suggests that their relationship as a couple is secondary to this telling of the story, and that Adam should be taken as a representative for all of humanity. The first and last verses of the passage indicate that the main theme of the story is the presence of divine forgiveness despite humanity's sin and weakness. The opening verse calls attention to human culpability by identifying Adam's offense as a refusal to follow the command—often stated in the Qur'an—that people should remember God. In response, God does not issue a threat as in Genesis ("In the day that you eat of it you shall die" Gen 2:17), but a reminder that Adam should be mindful. Adam has forgotten what God has told him (Q 20:115), but God accepts his remorse nonetheless (v. 122). The importance of this theme is reinforced by a comment on the consequences that await Adam if he fails to avoid Iblis (vv. 117–19). Despite that reminder, the couple falls short, as Iblis—in the guise of Satan—is able to deceive them (v. 120). As in chapter 7, Adam and Eve act together when they eat the fruit and one is not more at fault than the other (v. 121).

After the couple's offense, the deity does not sanction them in a way similar to the triple punishments directed at the serpent, Eve, and Adam described in Genesis (3:14–19). In place of such punishments the Qur'an makes use of three verbs to explain how God continues to support and provide for Adam despite his transgression: "Then his Lord chose him, returned to him with forgiveness, and guided him" (Q 20:122). The middle verb "return" (*tāba*) is particularly indicative of divine concern; it is sometimes used to describe the act of a person turning to God to ask forgiveness. In this way, the text expresses how the deity shows compassion to Adam, while simultaneously reminding the reader about what Adam's proper response to God should have been after he disregarded the command to not eat of the fruit. Like the version of the story in chapter 7, this one is also followed by a brief section that explains the universal application of its message (vv. 123b–24). The story of Adam's offense is related not solely to recount an event that took place in the long-ago past, but as a warning and reminder to later audiences that they should not follow the example of the first human being who failed to heed the call to remember God at all times.

The blame for his mistake is placed squarely on Adam's own shoulders, and the passage calls attention to the existence of human free will in a number of places. God warns the first human about the danger Iblis poses to him, and—to encourage Adam to follow that warning—the deity lays out for him the unpleasant consequences (hunger, nakedness, thirst, and unbearable heat) that will result from the wrong choice (vv. 117–19). Failure to heed God's warning will lead to a life of pain and misery outside the garden, while obedience to the divine will can extend their stay in comfort and peace. The choice is Adam's, and he opts for the path that will lead to suffering and distress.

The biblical Adam is also warned about what he should avoid, but that warning focuses on the threat of punishment: "And the LORD God commanded the man, 'You may freely eat of every tree of the garden; but of the tree of the knowledge of good and evil you shall not eat, for in the day that you eat of it you shall die'" (Gen 2:16–17). This stark warning lacks the warmth and concern of the counsel in the Qur'an, where God calls attention to the benefits of remaining in the garden and reveals to Adam the identity of the enemy from whom he must distance himself. The Genesis story conveys God's care for Adam and Eve in several details, and in that context this warning could be compared to a parent issuing a stern warning to a small child to avoid dangers like playing with matches. Still, in describing this warning the Qur'an presents a more caring image of a deity who attempts to convince Adam to do what is right by reasoning with him rather than simply pointing out the scary prospect of disobedience.

Another aspect of this version of the story also highlights the role of human free will. Unlike in the Qur'an's account in chapter 7, here Satan asks a question rather than making a statement (v. 120).[3] Adam must weigh his options and make a choice, and the text twice points to him as the guilty party so that he has no one to blame but himself (vv. 115, 121). Adam does not acknowledge his error or beg forgiveness as he and Eve do in the garden story of chapter 7. There is a reference to God accepting his repentance in verse 122, but the story downplays this element; the restoration of the relationship is due to divine initiative and the human side has less to do with it. In this way, the focus shifts toward the difference between God and humanity. While human actions can tend toward sin and error, the deity's actions tend only toward good, even to the point of guiding and showing mercy toward those who disobey the divine will.

Further Biblical Interpretations

The events of the garden story in Genesis 2—3 are not mentioned elsewhere in the Hebrew Bible, but the New Testament refers to them a few times. In the Letter to the Romans, Paul argues that Adam's actions were responsible for introducing sin and death into the world.

> [12]Therefore, just as sin came into the world through one man, and death came through sin, and so death spread to all because all have sinned—[13]sin was indeed in the world before the law, but sin is not reckoned when there is no law. [14]Yet death exercised dominion from Adam to Moses, even over those whose sins were not like the transgression of Adam, who is a type of the one who was to come....[18]Therefore just as one man's trespass led to condemnation for all, so one man's act of righteousness leads to justification and life for all. For just as by the one man's disobedience the many were made sinners, so by the one man's obedience the many will be made righteous. (Rom 5:12–14, 18–19)

In this passage Paul offers an interpretation that compares Jesus to Adam and explains how the events of Jesus's life rectified the harm done by Adam. This way of interpreting an Old Testament character as prefiguring one from the New Testament is called typology.

Genesis 2—3 offers some support for the idea that human mortality is a consequence of what Adam did (Gen 3:17–19), but with his claim that the first human's actions also resulted in sin that affects all humanity, Paul adds an element that is not found in the garden story. While Adam is told he will die, there is no indication that he committed a sin that was then passed down from one generation to the next. Paul, however, would have understood that in Hebrew the word *adam* can also designate humankind generally, which may explain why he does not refer to Eve here or in 1 Corinthians (discussed below). In Romans 5 Paul offers an interpretation of Genesis 2—3 that is meant to support his Christology, his understanding of who Jesus Christ is and what he accomplished. Paul's interpretation captures his conviction that what Jesus did has significance for all humanity, Gentiles as well as Jews; Christ's obedience unto death saved humanity from the condition of sin caused by Adam. Sin may be understood as being out of right relationship with God, and the salvation that Jesus accomplished, as bringing people into such right relationship.

Paul makes a similar interpretive move in 1 Corinthians. While this time he discusses Adam in light of Jesus's resurrection rather than the salvation that his death accomplished, the practical import is similar: new life in Christ brings one into right relationship with God. Just as Adam's death had universal implications, so too Jesus's defeat of death had an effect on all people: "For since death came through a human being, the resurrection of the dead has also come through a human being; for as all die in Adam, so all will be made alive in Christ" (1 Cor 15:21–22). The distinction between Adam and Jesus is further developed later in the same chapter: "The first man was from the earth, a man of dust; the second man is from heaven. As was the man of dust, so are those who are of the dust; and as is the man of heaven, so are those who are of heaven. Just as we have borne the image of the man of dust, we will also bear the image of the man of heaven" (1 Cor 15:47–49). Here, Paul's description of Adam makes a direct allusion to how he was created in Genesis (2:7; 3:19), and by calling attention to the different origins of Adam and Jesus, Paul highlights the superior status of Jesus.

Eve makes an appearance in Paul's other letter to the church of Corinth in a passage that expresses concern and warns them about people who are trying to pass themselves off as legitimate Christian leaders.

> [2]I feel a divine jealousy for you, for I promised you in marriage to one husband, to present you as a chaste

virgin to Christ. ³But I am afraid that as the serpent deceived Eve by its cunning, your thoughts will be led astray from a sincere and pure devotion to Christ. ⁴For if someone comes and proclaims another Jesus than the one we proclaimed, or if you receive a different spirit from the one you received, or a different gospel from the one you accepted, you submit to it readily enough. (2 Cor 11:2–4)

This is an obvious reference to the garden story, but as in the other two passages already discussed, an interpretive dimension is evident in how Paul is selective in employing the tradition. Adam's absence from the passage puts all the blame on Eve as the one responsible for the offense, and this does not accurately reflect what occurs in the Genesis story where Adam also eats the fruit. The focus on Eve is probably due to Paul's use of the marriage metaphor in verse 2 that presents the Corinthians in the role of a female spouse, but it results in an interpretation of the garden story that can support misogynistic readings of the text that place all the blame on Eve.

A final example of an interpretation of the garden story in the New Testament appears in 1 Timothy, a work that discusses roles and order within the Christian community. It cites Adam and Eve to support a patriarchal view of how men and women should relate to one another:

> ¹¹Let a woman learn in silence with full submission. ¹²I permit no woman to teach or to have authority over a man; she is to keep silent. ¹³For Adam was formed first, then Eve; ¹⁴and Adam was not deceived, but the woman was deceived and became a transgressor. ¹⁵Yet she will be saved through childbearing, provided they continue in faith and love and holiness, with modesty. (1 Tim 2:11–15).

The passage legitimates male superiority by tracing it back to the first couple, but it offers a less than accurate account of the events described in Genesis 2—3. Eve is presented as the one who was deceived and who transgressed, but that is also an apt description of Adam's role in the garden story. In addition, the passage states that women will be saved through childbearing, but in Genesis this is the means by which Eve is punished for her offense (3:19). The only element that the Genesis garden story supports in this passage is the fact that Adam was created first.

Focus for Comparison

Both the Qur'an and the New Testament interpret the Genesis garden story, and each does so to highlight themes central to its own message. The Islamic text presents the story in a way that calls attention to the boundless mercy of God. The deity is compassionate not only toward Adam and Eve, a couple who act in tandem and request God's forgiveness after they admit their mistake, but also toward Iblis/Satan, the enemy of humanity who convinces them to go against the divine will. The New Testament passages establish connections between Jesus and what happened in the garden. Adam and Eve do not set things right with God on their own, as they do in the Qur'an, and for Paul this results in an unbroken chain of human sin passed along from generation to generation. A "new Adam" is needed to save humanity. Through his death and resurrection, Jesus put an end to the cycle of sin and made available to all the divine mercy that the Qur'an's Adam and Eve experience in the garden.

Questions to Consider

1. How does the presence of Iblis/Satan have an impact on the garden story in the Qur'an?

2. How significant is it that the Qur'an sometimes identifies for the reader a story's key theme?

3. What themes do the biblical and qur'anic versions of the garden story have in common?

4. What is your reaction to the presence of more than one version of the garden story in the Qur'an?

5. How are the characters transformed in the Qur'an's interpretations of the garden story?

6. What are the main qualities of each character in the various versions of the garden story?

7. What is your response to how the New Testament interprets the Genesis garden story?

CHAPTER 3

Cain and Abel

As in the Bible, the story of the world's first murder in the Qur'an features the sons of Adam and Eve. There is only one account of the story in the Qur'an (5:27–32), and containing only six verses, it is briefer than the biblical version. The two passages have a number of things in common, but there are some important differences between them that show evidence of how the Islamic tradition interprets the biblical one. The most notable difference is the lack of narrative details in the Qur'an's description of the murder.

The First Murder

²⁷Tell them in truth the story of Adam's two sons.[1] When they presented an offering, it was accepted from one of them, but it was not accepted from the other. The one said, "Truly, I will kill you." The other said, "God accepts from the pious. ²⁸If you extend your hand against me to kill me, I will not extend mine to kill you. I fear God, the Lord of the universe. ²⁹I wish you would bear the sin committed against me and your other sins and be among the people of the fire, for that is the reward of those who are wrongdoers." ³⁰His mind aided him in the killing of his brother, so he killed him and became one of the lost ones. ³¹Then God sent a raven that scratched on the ground in order to show him how to bury his brother's corpse. He cried, "Woe is me! Am

I unable to be like this raven and bury my brother's corpse?" Then he became repentant. [32]Because of this We decreed for the children of Israel that whoever killed a person, except in the cases of punishment for murder or causing corruption in the land, it would be as if he had killed all people. And whoever saved a person, it would be as if he had saved all people. Our messengers came to them with clear signs, but even after that many of them have done evil in the land.

COMPARISON WITH THE BIBLICAL NARRATIVE

The biblical account of the murder is found in Genesis 4:1–16, and while the outcome is the same in both texts—in that one of the brothers takes the life of the other—the list below shows that there is not a great deal of overlap between them.

1. Sacrifice is accepted from one brother and not from the other. (Q 5:27a; Gen 4:3–5)
2. The murderer speaks to his brother. (Q 5:27b; Gen 4:8a)
3. One brother kills the other. (Q 5:30; Gen 4:8b)

Two of the five verses of the Qur'an story have a parallel in Genesis, and only four of the sixteen verses of the biblical account can be related to the Islamic version. The first and third of the three shared elements identify the key components at the heart of the plot—God's rejection of the sacrifice from one brother leads to the murder of the other. The second element, the murderer's speech, is present in both texts but, as we will see, its expanded form in the Qur'an demonstrates interpretation of the biblical tradition.

INTERPRETATION OF CAIN AND ABEL

The most obvious difference is the lack of details in the Qur'an passage. The first two verses of the biblical story provide background information about the brothers regarding their order of birth and their occupations. Genesis provides additional details by mentioning that Cain's offering to God consisted of fruit from the ground, while Abel brought the firstborn of his flock (Gen 4:3–4). The Qur'an does not convey any of this information and is also silent about something else regarding the brothers that Genesis mentions—their names. In the Hebrew text Cain is mentioned by name thirteen times and Abel is specifically identified seven times, while the Qur'an never refers to either by name. Other Muslim sources identify the brothers as Qabil and Habil, but in the Islamic scripture they are anonymous. All the reader knows about them from the Qur'an is their father's name and their relationship as brothers.

The lack of identifying characteristics leaves Cain and Abel less individualized in the Qur'an than they are in the Bible and so makes them representatives of types of people rather than unique individuals. The Bible's older sibling Cain, who works the land and brings vegetation to God, is now just a brother, and the biblical younger sibling Abel, who tends flocks and brings an animal for sacrifice, is simply another brother. What differentiates them in the Qur'an is what they say and do, not their birth order, occupations, offerings, or names. Through their actions and words the qur'anic brothers tell the reader what kind of people they are and represent, and the differences between them could not be more extreme—the murdered one is an innocent victim who places his trust in God, while the murderer is guilty because he relies on himself. The anonymity of the brothers serves another purpose found in the Qur'an's presentation of a number of biblical figures and events: to enable the reader to focus better on the intended message. The passage does not recount the story of two brothers named Cain and Abel who lived long ago; rather, it contains a lesson about two types of people that has present-day relevance for anyone reading the text.

Turning to the role of God, the plot in both texts gets moving as the deity accepts the sacrifice from one brother and rejects it from the other. The two texts differ in describing this action in that God is specifically mentioned only in the biblical account, while in the Qur'an the passive voice is used: "It was accepted from one of them, but it was not accepted from the other" (v. 27). Yet, that the murdered brother goes on to say, "God accepts from the pious" indicates that the deity is the one doing the accepting and rejecting, even though the text does not explicitly say so.

More significant for the difference in the portrayal of God is that the Genesis story has God speak to Cain prior to the murder and lay out the two options before him. "The LORD said to Cain, 'Why are you angry, and why has your countenance fallen? If you do well, will you not be accepted? And if you do not do well, sin is lurking at the door; its desire is for you, but you must master it'" (Gen 4:6–7). With these words, God reminds Cain to avoid evil, and so the deity plays a more prominent role in this part of the biblical story. The encounter with God in the Bible puts Cain in an even more negative light because when he kills Abel, the act can be interpreted as a rejection of God's advice to him that expresses his disobedience toward the divine will.

Despite its relative lack of narrative detail, the Qur'an contains certain information not present in Genesis. In particular, it describes a conversation between the two brothers that takes place just prior to the murder. The biblical account has a similar scene, but it is not a conversation. Cain does all the talking and has only one line. "Cain said to his brother Abel, 'Let us go out to the field'" (Gen 4:8a).[2] The Qur'an, on the other hand, reports a full conversation between the two brothers. Abel, who never speaks in the Bible, has much more to say than Cain does in the Islamic tradition (Q 5:27b–29).

Cain speaks only one line to his brother as in the Bible, but in the Qur'an it is not an ambiguous statement open to misunderstanding. His invitation in Genesis to go into the field could be interpreted by Abel or the reader in any number of ways, but that is not the case in the Qur'an, since the words "I will kill you" can be taken only one way. It therefore remains an open question as to whether or not the biblical Abel was caught off guard and unprepared when Cain attacked him, but there is no doubt that his counterpart in the Qur'an would have seen it coming.

The qur'anic Abel responds to Cain's threat in an unexpected way. Rather than seek an explanation for his brother's aggressive attitude or react in kind, he shifts the topic to belief in God. He first clarifies why his sacrifice was accepted but Cain's was not, pointing out that only offerings that are brought by those who are mindful of God are worthy of acceptance. The Arabic term here for "pious" (*muttaqīn*) is used nearly fifty times in the Qur'an to express the devotion that one should have toward God.[3] Abel demonstrates his own reverence for the deity in the next verse when he says, "I fear God" (v. 28), thereby including himself among the mindful whose sacrifices are accepted. Fear of God does not imply terror before a malevolent deity, but rather an attitude of awe and reverence before God, who cannot be manipulated. Such fear is also celebrated in the Bible as a hallmark of the true believer, and so it provides an important point of contact between the two texts concerning the proper attitude toward God.[4] Abel refers to God using the title "Lord of the universe" (*rabb al-ʿālamīn*), a phrase used more than forty times in the Qur'an to designate the deity as having authority over all that exists. Here this title is among the last words Abel utters prior to his death at his brother's hand and so gives the text a distinctly Islamic flavor.[5]

In addition to his relationship with God, Abel addresses his relationship with Cain. He first assures him that he will not defend himself or counterattack if his brother should try to harm him (v. 28). He then states his wish that Cain should be burdened with "the sin committed against me and your other sins" and enter hellfire (v. 29). With these words he is not suggesting that his brother should somehow take upon himself any sins that Abel has committed during his lifetime and be held responsible for them. Rather, Abel is more likely referring to the sin that Cain will be guilty of if he should take his brother's life. The Qur'an contains a number of graphic descriptions of hell that stress the pain and suffering its inhabitants endure, and Abel's wish that this be his brother's fate highlights the deep divisions between him and Cain and the fractured nature of their relationship.[6]

Cain and Abel do not have a conversation like this in Genesis, but their exchange plays a similar role to the encounter Cain has with God in the Bible prior to killing Abel (Gen 4:6–7). In both cases, Cain is confronted with a choice he must make as he struggles with how to respond to the rejection of his offering. God presents the alternatives before him in stark terms in the biblical account—if he acts properly all will turn out well, but if he acts improperly he will be controlled by sin. In the Qur'an Abel is not as blunt, but his words nonetheless imply that Cain has a choice to make—Cain can either join him among the ranks of the mindful ones who fear God, or he can give in to his own selfish desires and align himself with the denizens of hell. In both texts Cain can exercise his free will as he chooses. By reminding Cain of the choice that confronts him prior to the murder, God plays a more active role in the biblical version than in the Qur'an, but that does not mean the deity is a nonfactor in the Islamic text. Abel's words to Cain are full of theological language with their references to God's acceptance of the pious, fear of God, and hellfire, and so the activity of the deity is implied rather than described explicitly.

The lack of explicit description of God's action in the qur'anic story prior to the murder shifts the attention to the brothers. As already noted, the fact that they have been shorn of all individuality allows them to take on a more symbolic role, representing two different types of people. Consequently, in the Qur'an this becomes a story about the choices that every person, not just Cain and Abel, must confront and make. The victim is a faithful believer who puts all of his trust in God. He says as much by identifying himself as one who is pious and fears God. The killer represents those who make the opposite choice. He is a faithless unbeliever who takes matters into his own hands and is incapable of submitting to the divine will. The two brothers do have clearly defined separate identities in the Qur'an, but these are not established through social or cultural categories like names, occupations, or types of sacrifices, as they are in Genesis. It is rather along theological lines that the Islamic text distinguishes the brothers, with one expressing his faith in God and the other relying on himself.

The Qur'an is also more specific about why Cain took his brother's life. Genesis makes a reference to his anger and fallen countenance after his offering is rejected (4:5), but the biblical narrative offers no precise motivation for the murder. In contrast, the Qur'an says specifically what caused the bloodshed when it states, "His mind aided him in the killing of his brother" (v. 30a). The word translated as "mind" (*nafs*) comes from an Arabic root whose basic meaning is "to breathe." The root does not carry this exact sense in the Qur'an, where it appears almost three hundred times and usually refers to a person or some aspect of a person. Among the many meanings it conveys in the text are "life," "self," "person," and "soul." These senses are quite close to one another, and that complicates any attempt to determine what the term means in this passage. It can on occasion refer to one's reason or intellect, and if we adopt that alternative another possible translation would be "mind." This can be contrasted with the biblical account when God warns Cain, "Sin is lurking at the door; its desire is for you, but you must master it" (Gen 4:7). The Bible emphasizes the external threat of sin combined with the need to master it, but the Qur'an stresses only the internal threat of Cain making a poor choice.

The story ends much differently in the Bible than it does in the Qur'an, for Cain at least. After Abel's death in Genesis, the conversation between God and Cain resumes and the deity confronts him about what he has done. When questioned on Abel's whereabouts, Cain is decidedly evasive and utters one of the most famous lines in the entire Bible, "I do not know; am I my brother's keeper?" (Gen 4:9b). He never actually admits to killing his brother in the Bible and does not express remorse for the act, but in his conversation with God he makes clear his awareness of his guilt. After God punishes him by making him a fugitive and wanderer on earth, no longer able to work the land, Cain fears for his life and believes all who meet him will want to kill him. Showing him a degree of mercy, God prevents that from happening by putting on him the "mark of Cain" that will prevent any harm coming to him (Gen 4:15). According to Genesis, Cain spent the rest of his days away from God's presence in the land of Nod, east of Eden, where he had a son named Enoch (4:17).

The qur'anic Cain is self-reflective in a way that his biblical counterpart is not, as is apparent primarily in the episode involving the raven,[7] which is not recorded in Genesis. When he sees the bird scratching on the ground, Cain realizes that he has not buried his brother's corpse and he expresses regret (v. 31). The Arabic root that describes Cain's reaction (*nadima*) is always used in the Qur'an to depict the remorse a person or group feels after either doing something they should not have done or not doing something they should have, and it typically implies a degree of repentance. While the passage does not state that he feels regret for having killed him, it indicates that Cain is remorseful about not properly burying his brother's body, acknowledging an obligation to treat Abel's remains with dignity and respect. The biblical Cain never expresses any remorse or misgivings about his actions.

By becoming repentant, the Cain of the Qur'an takes personal responsibility for what he has done and, unlike his counterpart in Genesis, remembers that he is in fact his brother's keeper.

While not present in the Bible, this scene has a parallel in extrabiblical Jewish literature. Some sources, like the Targum of Jeremiah, report that after Abel's death Adam and Eve were at a loss as to what to do with their son's body.[8] A raven suddenly appeared and began to peck at the ground in order to cover up the body of another bird that had died. At that point, Adam and Eve realized that this would be an appropriate way to dispose of Abel's corpse and so they did as the bird had done. The Targum cites the raven tradition as an explanation for the practice of burial, while the Qur'an uses it to make an important point about Cain's remorse at his inability to properly take care of his brother's remains.

A key aspect of the Islamic text is the role God plays in sending the raven to Cain. The deity is explicitly mentioned three times in the passage, with the other two occurrences coming in Abel's conversation with Cain (vv. 27, 28). God never utters a word or speaks to either brother throughout the story. This is the only time God acts explicitly in the entire passage, and it is a significant action because the sending of the bird is what enables Cain to recognize his error and express his repentance. But Cain is unaware of God's role in sending the raven, as he thinks he came to this insight on his own when he observed the bird and interpreted what its actions meant. The text shows that God set the events in motion that made possible Cain's realization and subsequent rehabilitation. This passage offers a clear example of how the Islamic text interprets the biblical tradition to convey a recurrent qur'anic theme: God is the supreme authority over all of creation, and everything that occurs in the world is subject to that authority. Everything submits to the divine will, even when God's presence or involvement is not immediately apparent. The raven exemplifies this submission when it responds obediently to God's command to go to Cain and scratch on the ground, and Cain also exemplifies it by then expressing remorse for what he has done.

God exerts authority in the biblical story by cursing Cain, sending him away, and giving him a sign that will prevent others from harming him (Gen 4:11–16). Cain can do nothing but submit to each of these acts of divine power. But the outcome of his submission is strikingly different in the two texts. The Cain of Genesis knowingly surrenders to God's authority as he acknowledges that what the deity has commanded will come to pass when he says, "Today you have driven me away from the soil, and I shall be hidden from your face; I shall be a fugitive and a wanderer on the earth, and anyone who meets me may kill me" (Gen 4:14). But that submission is also a form of resignation because Cain has no choice but to accept his fate and live out his days as an unrepentant murderer who is alienated from the world and God. The Cain of the Qur'an, on the other hand, unknowingly expresses a submission to God's will that has enabled him to take ownership of what he has done by repenting, and this opens up the possibility of an improved relationship with God and the world.

Those divergent paths for Cain can be seen in the different ways the ground functions in the two texts. In Genesis, it condemns Cain and is closely tied to the punishment he will receive for his evil deed:

> ¹⁰And the LORD said, "What have you done? Listen; your brother's blood is crying out to me from the ground! ¹¹And now you are cursed from the ground, which has opened its mouth to receive your brother's blood from your hand. ¹²When you till the ground, it will no longer yield to you its strength; you will be a fugitive and a wanderer on the earth." (Gen 4:10–12)

In the space of three verses the term "ground" appears three times and the word "earth" once, and in each case they implicate Cain and execute judgement against him. In the Qur'an, however, the ground plays a role not in Cain's condemnation but in his repentance. The moment when Cain sees the raven scratching on the ground is the turning point that allows him to admit his error and become a model of repentance.

The Qur'an also interprets the tradition by including a coda that identifies why the story of Cain and Abel has been related. The Islamic text commonly calls attention to the main teaching of a given passage, and after the conclusion of this story a comment explains the origin of Jewish legislation regarding the taking of human life (v. 32). A similar statement is made in an authoritative extrabiblical Jewish source, the Mishnah, a written collection of previously oral Jewish legal traditions from the end of the second century CE. A passage from that text attempts to explain a grammatical anomaly in the Genesis story. After the murder God says to Cain, "Your brother's blood is crying out to me from the ground" (Gen 4:10), but the Hebrew text has the plural form of the word *blood*. The Mishnah states that the plural is used because it refers to both the blood of Abel and that of his offspring, and then it goes on to say that those who kill a single Israelite will be treated as if they had killed the entire human race, and those who save an individual Israelite will be treated as though they have preserved all people.[9] The term *blood* does not appear in the Qur'an story, but the entire episode of Abel's death is directly tied to the universal implications of a single murder.

The last sentence of verse 32 also exhibits evidence of Islamic interpretation. The lack of success on the part of messengers sent by God is a frequent theme in the Qur'an, and it likely speaks to the negative response the Prophet Muhammad received when he delivered his message in seventh-century Arabia. The prophetic paradigm repeated throughout the Qur'an describes prior prophets who were rejected by their contemporaries, and this is a way the text attempts to validate Muhammad's role as a prophet. According to the Qur'an, God's messengers were consistently rejected by the people to whom they were sent, and so Muhammad's experience of rejection is a legitimation of his prophetic status.

Further Biblical Interpretations

As is the case with the garden story in Genesis 2—3, Cain's murder of Abel is not mentioned anywhere else in the Hebrew Bible. Nonetheless, the brothers do make an anonymous appearance in the Wisdom of Solomon, a work written in the late first century BCE or early first century CE that is included in the canonical Bible for Roman Catholic and Eastern Orthodox Christians.[10] In the tenth chapter of that book the unnamed brothers are cited in a summary of the events described in the first nine chapters of Genesis.

¹Wisdom protected the first-formed father of the world,
   when he alone had been created;
she delivered him from his transgression,
²and gave him strength to rule all things.
³But when an unrighteous man departed from her in his
   anger,
he perished because in rage he killed his brother.
⁴When the earth was flooded because of him, wisdom again
   saved it,
steering the righteous man by a paltry piece of wood.
   (Wis 10:1–4)

The passage describes Cain as unrighteous because of his having rejected wisdom. Like other wisdom writings (e.g., Job, Ecclesiastes, Proverbs), the Wisdom of Solomon privileges wisdom as an essential quality of human life that will enable one to live properly and in conformity with God's will. The idea that his abandonment of wisdom led Cain to kill Abel—an observation missing in the Genesis account—corresponds with the theological perspective of the Wisdom of Solomon, which, like the Qur'an, has interpreted the tradition to support its own viewpoint.

The same can be said about two other things the Wisdom of Solomon says about Cain that are not present in Genesis. According to verse 3b, Cain died because he killed Abel in a fit of rage, an assertion that does not match what Genesis says. If the Wisdom of Solomon is attempting to explain why Cain died at all, this ignores the fact that death was already introduced with Adam and Eve. If it is claiming that he died because he was killed in retaliation for the murder he committed, this too does not square with Genesis. When Cain expresses concern that others will try to kill him, God intervenes by placing the mark of Cain upon him and warning anyone who would harm him, "Whoever kills Cain will suffer a sevenfold vengeance" (Gen 4:15a). Therefore, his death did not come about because of his murderous act, and God even takes measures to guarantee that Cain will not suffer the same fate as his brother. Genesis does not report how old Cain was when he died, but he lived long enough to father a child and build a city (Gen 4:17), so the cause-and-effect relationship between Abel's death and Cain's that is suggested by the Wisdom of Solomon is not backed up by Genesis.

The passage from the Wisdom of Solomon goes on to blame Cain for the flood God sent during Noah's time (v. 4a), and to attribute to wisdom the saving of all in the ark (v. 4b). Neither observation is reported in the flood story (Gen 6—9), where Cain is not mentioned and the cause of the flood is identified without implicating Cain. "The LORD saw that the wickedness of human-kind was great in the earth, and that every inclination of the thoughts of their hearts was only evil continually" (Gen 6:5; cf. Gen 6:11–12). This general condemnation of humanity does not single out any one character, and Cain's offense is simply the first in a succession that continues with that of Lamech (Gen 4:18–24) and on through succeeding generations until the flood. Nor does Genesis mention the role of wisdom in guiding the ark through the storm. In both of these respects the tradition has been interpreted to support the perspective of the Wisdom of Solomon.

The New Testament's First Letter of John also puts forward a cause for Abel's murder. "For this is the message you have heard from the beginning, that we should love one another. We must not be like Cain who was from the evil one and murdered his brother. And why did he murder him? Because his own deeds were evil and his brother's righteous" (1 John 3:11–12). The author has added some elements that are lacking in the Genesis account. Describing Cain as being from "the evil one" is an allusion to Satan, but no mention of Satan or the devil is made in Genesis 4. Similarly, while 1 John distinguishes between Cain's evil deeds and Abel's righteous ones, in Genesis neither brother's actions are explicitly defined or labeled with these terms. As does the Wisdom of Solomon, 1 John interprets the Cain and Abel story to undergird the author's view-point. This letter adopts a parental tone by which the author seeks to instruct the readers about how to relate to one another, and they are often referred to as "brothers and sisters" and "little chil-dren." The fraternal relationship between Cain and Abel suits this purpose very well, and by presenting the former's actions as evil and the latter's as righteous, the two characters represent types of people the reader should avoid and emulate, respectively. Beyond this passage the letter makes several references to the evil one or

Satan (2:13, 14; 3:8, 10), and so the identification of the evil one as Cain's origin aligns well with the author's message.

Four New Testament passages mention Abel as a model for Christians. In the Letter to the Hebrews, a work from the second half of the first century written to encourage early Christians to remain faithful, chapter 11 discusses the faith of important people from the past. That discussion cites Abel's sacrifice. "By faith Abel offered to God a more acceptable sacrifice than Cain's. Through this he received approval as righteous, God himself giving approval to his gifts; he died, but through his faith he still speaks" (Heb 11:4). The Genesis narrative does not say anything about Abel's faith (other than the offering he makes) or his righteousness, but the author of Hebrews associates him with these themes to establish the pattern that will be repeated in the lives of Enoch, Abraham, Moses, and other venerable figures throughout the rest of the chapter (Heb 11:5–40). Because his faith plays a significant role in the Qur'an, this interpretation of Abel resonates with the Islamic text.

The blood of Abel is a key motif in the other three passages, two of which occur in a speech presented in Matthew and Luke. In the Gospel of Matthew Jesus reprimands the scribes and Pharisees by associating them with the death of Abel, who is identified as righteous there as well.

> [34]Therefore I send you prophets, sages, and scribes, some of whom you will kill and crucify, and some you will flog in your synagogues and pursue from town to town, [35]so that upon you may come all the righteous blood shed on earth, from the blood of righteous Abel to the blood of Zechariah son of Barachiah, whom you murdered between the sanctuary and the altar. (Matt 23:34–35)

In his version of the same speech Luke does not call Abel righteous, but he identifies him as a prophet (Luke 11:49–51). Many figures who do not have the title in the Bible are prophets in the Qur'an, but Abel is not one of them. Luke's use of the prophet theme here is due to the way in which he presents Jesus as a prophet who must die (Luke 13:31–35).

A passage in Hebrews refers to Abel's blood as inferior to that of Jesus in order to underscore the unique significance of what Jesus accomplished.

> [22]But you have come to Mount Zion and to the city of the living God, the heavenly Jerusalem, and to innumerable angels in festal gathering, [23]and to the assembly of the firstborn who are enrolled in heaven, and to God the judge of all, and to the spirits of the righteous made perfect, [24]and to Jesus, the mediator of a new covenant, and to the sprinkled blood that speaks a better word than the blood of Abel. (Heb 12:22–24)

This passage offers another example of the interpretive process at work. Abel's blood does not have a negative connotation in the Genesis story, but within the context of the Christian text of Hebrews it is viewed less positively. The implication here is that Abel's blood is inferior because it called out for vengeance and punishment after his death, while Jesus's bloodshed led to forgiveness and reconciliation. In this way the Letter to the Hebrews invites readers to reflect on the transformed relationship with God that is available to them through faith in Jesus.

Focus for Comparison

Each of the New Testament passages that interpret the Cain and Abel tradition focuses on only one of the brothers. The faith and blood of Abel are mentioned in some of them, while another emphasizes Cain's evil actions and the role Satan played in causing him to kill his brother. One passage compares the blood of Abel with that of Jesus in order to cultivate readers' faith in Jesus. The Qur'an's interpretation of the tradition depersonalizes the brothers so that the only thing setting them apart is that one is a believer and the other is not. The qur'anic account also highlights the role of free will and portrays Cain's character repenting for the murder of his brother. This opens up the possibility that, like most biblical characters in the Qur'an, he will experience God's mercy and forgiveness.

Questions to Consider

1. What are the most important differences in the ways that God is presented in the versions of the stories in Genesis and in the Qur'an?

2. What relevance does the biblical account of the story have for modern readers?

3. What are some of the possible reasons why God rejected Cain's sacrifice in Genesis?

4. What do the different meanings of the Arabic word *nafs* suggest about what prompted Cain to kill Abel?

5. Is God more merciful in one of the versions of the story?

6. What are your thoughts about how the Cain and Abel story is interpreted elsewhere in the biblical literature?

CHAPTER 4

Noah and His Family

The flood that occurred during Noah's time is mentioned in eight passages in the Qur'an, each presenting him as someone sent by God to warn his people about the coming disaster. The following passage recounts what took place before the flood, highlighting Noah's role as a messenger:

> [59]We sent Noah to his people, and he said, "Oh my people, worship God! There is no other god for you than Him. Truly, I fear for you the punishment of a terrible day." [60]The leaders of his people said, "Surely, we see that you are in clear error." [61]He replied, "Oh my people, there is no error in me, but I am a messenger from the Lord of the universe. [62]I bring to you the messages of my Lord, and I advise you. I know things from God that you do not know. [63]Are you surprised that a reminder from your Lord has come to you from a man among you that he might warn you so you will be pious and then treated mercifully?" [64]But they called him a liar, so We saved him and those with him in the ark, and We drowned those who rejected Our signs. They were truly a blind people. (Q 7:59–64)

The flood itself is hardly mentioned in this passage because the emphasis is on Noah's role as a prophet and his people's inability to accept him as such. Noah does not have prophetic status in the Bible as he does in the Qur'an, and this is one way the Islamic text interprets the biblical tradition. As with other prophets from the past, the Qur'an highlights the rejection Noah experienced, and this establishes a framework within which Muhammad's life can be understood. Muhammad's message was also shunned by many of his contemporaries and, like Noah and others before Muhammad, he was called a liar (Q 11:35; 21:5; 46:8). Noah's question about the people's inability to accept one of their own bringing a message from God (v. 63) is one that Muhammad might have posed in seventh-century Arabia. In this way, Noah helps to validate Muhammad's status as a prophet.

The Flood Story

Another qur'anic passage (Q 11:25–49) begins in a similar way, but then goes on to describe events that took place during the flood.[1] The account can be divided into three sections, which are marked off in the translation by the spaces before and after verse 35.

[25]We sent Noah to his people [saying], "I am a clear warner to you [26]that you worship none but God. I fear for you the punishment of a painful day." [27]The unfaithful leaders of his people said, "We see you as nothing but a human being like ourselves, and we see that the only ones who follow you are the vilest among us. We do not see you to be better than we are, but we think you are liars." [28]He said, "Oh my people, do you think that, if I have firm evidence from my Lord and He has granted me mercy but it has remained unapparent to you, we should force it upon you while you are averse to it? [29]Oh my people, I do not ask you for any payment in return for it since my reward is only God. I am not going to drive away those who believe. Surely they will meet their Lord. But I see you are an ignorant people. [30]Oh my people, who would aid me against God if I were to drive them away? Will you not remember? [31]I do not tell you that I possess God's treasures or that I know what is hidden. I do not say I am an angel, nor do

I say about those whom you hold in contempt that God will not grant them anything good. God knows what is in their souls. Truly, if I did that I would be among the evildoers." [32]They said, "Oh Noah, you have argued with us long and hard. Bring on us what you threaten us with, if you are among the truthful." [33]He said, "God will bring it upon you, if He wishes, and you cannot escape. [34]My advice will not be of use to you, even if I wish to advise you, if God wants to lead you astray. He is your Lord, and to Him you shall be made to return."

[35]Do they say, "He has fabricated it"? Say [Muhammad], "If I have fabricated it may my guilt be upon me, but I am innocent of the crimes you commit."

[36]It was revealed to Noah, "None of your people will believe except those who have already believed, so do not be bothered by what they are doing. [37]Build the ark under Our eyes and under Our inspiration. Do not speak to Me about those who have done wrong, for they will be drowned." [38]He made the ark, and the leaders of his people mocked him whenever they passed by. He said, "If you mock us we shall eventually mock you as you are now mocking. Then you will know upon whom a shameful punishment will come. A painful punishment will settle upon him." [40]When Our command came and the fountains gushed forth, We said, "Load on it a pair of every kind and your family, except for the one against whom the word has already gone forth, and whoever believes." But only a few believed with him. [41]He said, "Get on! May its mooring and sailing be in the name of God. My Lord is truly the forgiving and merciful One." [42]It made its way with them through waves like mountains. Noah cried out to his son, who was standing apart, "Oh son, get on with us and do not be with the unbelievers." [43]He replied, "I will take refuge on a mountain that will save me from the water." Noah said, "There is no protection today from the decree of God except for the one to whom He shows mercy." A wave came between them and he

was among the drowned. ⁴⁴Then it was said, "Oh earth, swallow your water! Oh earth, desist!" The water subsided and the matter was decided. The ark came to rest on Mount Judi and it was said, "A curse upon the evildoers!" ⁴⁵Noah cried out to his Lord and said, "Lord, my son is of my family! Surely, Your promise is true and You are the most just of judges." ⁴⁶He said, "Oh, Noah, he is not of your family, but he is unrighteous. Do not ask me about that of which you have no knowledge. I admonish you not to be one of the ignorant." ⁴⁷He said, "Lord, I seek Your protection for asking You about what I have no knowledge of. Unless you forgive me and show me mercy, I will be among the lost ones." ⁴⁸It was said, "Oh Noah, disembark with peace from Us and blessings upon you and upon the peoples of those with you. We shall provide for other peoples and then a painful punishment from Us will befall them." ⁴⁹This is part of the tidings We reveal to you [Muhammad]. You did not know it before this, nor did your people. Be patient, for the end is for the pious. (Q 11:25–49)

COMPARISON WITH THE BIBLICAL NARRATIVE

The following are the most significant elements that this Qur'an passage shares with the biblical flood story related in Genesis 6:5—9:29.

1. Noah is commanded by God to build the ark. (Gen 6:14–16; Q 11:37)
2. Animals and Noah's family members are saved. (Gen 6:18–20; Q 11:40)
3. Water comes up from underneath the earth. (Gen 7:11; Q 11:40)
4. Noah is told to board the ark. (Gen 7:1; Q 11:41)
5. The ark settles on a mountain. (Gen 8:4; Q 11:44)
6. God tells Noah to leave the ark. (Gen 8:15–16; Q 11:48)

While this outline indicates that the two versions share the same general narrative framework, they have very few details in common. For example, Noah's family members are presented differently in the Bible and the Qur'an. The Genesis text suggests that all of Noah's relatives were saved on the ark, but in the Qur'an his son loses his life when he refuses to get on board. Similarly, the place where the ark comes to rest is identified somewhat differently; the mount's name is Judi in the Qur'an (v. 44),[2] but Genesis refers to the location as "the mountains of Ararat" (8:4). The Bible also provides information the Qur'an does not include about the material that is to be used to build the ark, its dimensions, and the layout of the vessel (Gen 6:14–16).

Comparing the size and narrative flow of the two versions, at ninety-three verses the Genesis account is much longer than the qur'anic one,[3] and the bulk of the biblical story covers the period of time after Noah is instructed to build the ark. Less than 10 percent of the Genesis text treats events prior to the construction of the ark, but the first half of the Qur'an's version is devoted to that time period. The entirety of that first half of the Qur'an passage describes Noah's conversation with his people as they mock him and express their lack of belief in his message, whereas such an encounter is not reported in Genesis.[4] In other words, the Qur'an spends an equal amount of time on both the period prior to the flood and the flood itself, but 90 percent of the biblical passage treats the latter. The following discussion takes up each of the three sections of the passage and concludes with overall observations.

INTERPRETATION OF NOAH

First section

As already noted, the first section (vv. 25–34) takes the form of an extended conversation between Noah and the people, in which he appeals to them to worship only God (v. 26). This implies that they are worshiping more than the one God and are therefore guilty of the sin of polytheism or "association," as were many of the other peoples to whom earlier prophets were sent. In Islam, association (*shirk*) refers to the act of associating something or someone in creation with the uncreated deity in a way that violates the unity of

God.[5] After that brief command to worship only God, the rest of the section relates a conversation between Noah and the people in which he tries to defend himself against their accusations that he is not a legitimate envoy from God. Noah refers to himself as "a warner" (v. 25; *nadhīr*), a term that is commonly used to describe Muhammad in the Qur'an.[6] In fact, Muhammad and Noah are the only two named individuals to be called a warner in the Qur'an. By contrast, Noah is never identified as a warner in Genesis.

Noah's role as a warner in the Qur'an becomes apparent through the great amount of talking he does. He is the subject of ten verbs throughout this entire passage, and all but one relate to his speaking. The only exception recounts his building the ark (v. 38). To properly understand the Islamic Noah's character, we must pay attention to what he says. This is not the case in the biblical account, where Noah utters only one line; after the flood's waters have subsided and he is back on dry land, he curses the offspring of one of his sons (Gen 9:25–27).[7] In the Bible it is Noah's actions that define him, and they present him as an obedient person because he does everything that God asks him to do.

The way his relationship with the people is highlighted in the Qur'an also calls attention to Noah's identity as a prophet who warns. In three consecutive verses of this section he addresses them as "my people" (vv. 28–30), and in four other places they are described as "his" or "your" people (vv. 25, 27, 36, 38). This designation is in line with Islamic teaching regarding the prophets of the past, each of whom was sent to his own people to deliver a message. The seven references to Noah and his people in the space of fourteen verses underscore that relationship. Here, too, the contrast with the biblical version is striking because it does not refer to Noah's people a single time.

Second section

The one-verse middle section (v. 35) is directed to Muhammad. This type of sudden shift from reporting events of the past to directing a comment to Muhammad occurs occasionally in the Qur'an.[8] In the present case, the comment is strategically located because, while it breaks the flow of the story, it also highlights the association between Noah and Muhammad. His prophetic predecessor has just had a conversation with his people that ends with Noah telling them that they will be held accountable by God for rejecting him. This verse is a reminder that the prophet of Islam has experienced similar treatment from his own people, and it also calls attention to their wrongdoing. If the verse were removed, the two larger sections before and after it would smoothly follow one after the other, but its inclusion calls attention to the larger purpose of the passage as the retelling of events in the life of an earlier prophet to legitimate Muhammad's role as a messenger.

Third section

The third section (vv. 36–49) reports the building of the ark, the flood, and its aftermath. In both the Qur'an and the Bible only a small number of people are saved from the flood, but the two texts do not agree on who they are. In Genesis it is only Noah and his immediate family who enter the ark, and they are identified as his wife, his sons, and his sons' wives. Elsewhere his three sons' names are given as Shem, Ham, and Japheth (Gen 5:32; 9:18–27; 10:1). The biblical story specifies that Noah was the only righteous person on the earth at the time (Gen 7:1), and this suggests that the other members of his family were saved simply because they were related to him. According to verse 40 of the Qur'an passage, the passengers on the ark included other people besides Noah's family. This verse gives us some important information: (1) there was a small number of nonfamily members on the vessel; (2) only believers were saved; (3) the family members on the ark were believers; and (4) not all of Noah's family members were believers.

The fate of Noah's son is anticipated with the reference to "the one against whom the word has already gone forth" (v. 40). It is also foreshadowed in the first two verses of the section. The death of the son suggests that the rest of Noah's family was righteous because, if they were not, they would have drowned with the others. Noah's son represents unbelievers who persist in their lack of faith and are unable to submit to God's will. Noah attempts to persuade him to board the ark and not stay with those who lack faith, but his son stubbornly refuses and prefers to seek refuge on a mountain that he thinks will protect him. Ironically, if he had taken his father's advice he would have ended up on a different mountain, the one the ark came to rest on, and he would have been spared. The Arabic root for the verb "to take refuge" (*'aṣama*) that the son uses occurs elsewhere in the Qur'an, and a recurring theme in those passages is that God is the only thing people should cling to and take refuge in (Q 3:101; 4:146, 175; 22:78). Noah's son exercises his free will and makes the choice to hold fast to something other than God, and he pays for that decision with his life.

This tragic episode acknowledges that even a prophet's son can make the wrong choice, and it teaches that one cannot be saved on the basis of one's family ties. In fact, this passage indicates that blood relationships are sometimes meaningless and that dependence on them must be replaced with another way of thinking. In the conversation between Noah and God after the son's death, the deity puts forward a completely new definition of family (vv. 45–46). Noah wrestles with the seeming inconsistency that God is fair and just yet allows Noah's offspring to die. God responds by telling him that he is mistaken because his son, although he was his flesh and blood, was not a member of Noah's family. God challenges the prophet to think about family as a religious category rather than a physical one. He should not define familial relationships along the lines of biology, but shift the basis for family to shared belief. One's true family members are fellow believers rather than those who share the same ancestors.

This new way of thinking about what constitutes a family would have had great relevance for the early Muslim community. Muhammad's message was not well received by the people of Mecca when he first began to urge them to embrace monotheism. Some of them heeded his call, but according to Muslim sources most did not. Those who chose to follow Muhammad often did so at great personal cost, including alienation from friends and relatives who did not become Muslims. Qur'an passages like this one speak to those circumstances and attempt to encourage believers to remain faithful to Islam despite the many hardships they might encounter. The story of Noah and his son is meant to be a lesson for Muslims regarding the social groups with which they identify and that give meaning to their lives. Family in the biological sense is highly valued in the Qur'an and Islam, but in some situations it must be reconceived and reimagined.[9]

By challenging God on the death of his son, Noah is not acting like a good prophet, and the response of the deity is worth noting. God does not punish Noah but rather puts him in his place by reminding him that some things are beyond his understanding (v. 46). The warner has been warned. This leads Noah to admit his mistake and beg for God's pardon (v. 47). In this scene Noah must practice what he has been preaching and accept the divine will even though it is beyond his comprehension and has caused him deep personal grief. This distinguishes Noah from his son and his people—he surrenders his own will to a power greater than himself, something they are not capable of doing. The conversation between Noah and God ends with the deity extending to him the forgiveness he seeks. The mercy of God is a central theme of the Qur'an, and many texts like this one demonstrate that all one needs to do to experience God's forgiveness is to repent and ask for it.[10]

God's final words to Noah in the Qur'an passage highlight an important difference between it and the biblical version regarding the portrayal of the deity (v. 48). God blesses Noah as he leaves the ark and extends that blessing to some of his offspring as well. At the same time, the deity asserts that Noah will have other descendants who will be less deserving of that reward, and they will suffer the consequences for how they live their lives. With these words, God acknowledges the presence of human sin on the part of some but places it within the context of others who will be rewarded and blessed because they are good people.

This is quite different from the way the biblical flood story ends. After Noah leaves the ark he offers a sacrifice to God that causes the deity to say, "I will never again curse the ground because of humankind, for the inclination of the human heart is evil from youth; nor will I ever again destroy every living creature as I have done" (Gen 8:21). In this verse God expresses, without qualification, a negative view of human beings as creatures who are flawed from birth and throughout their lives have a propensity toward evil and sin. This blanket observation about the evil inclination of humanity resembles the one that prompted God to enact the flood in the first place (Gen 6:5, 11–13). As such, it raises a question about how effective the flood was in addressing the problem God hoped to solve with it. If things are more or less the same after the deluge as before it, what was the point of sending it in the first place? The answer lies not in the flood story itself, but in the narrative trajectory of the Pentateuch. It is from the descendants of the righteous Noah that God eventually chooses the people of Israel with whom to establish a covenant, giving them instructions, the Torah of Moses, by which to live in right relationship with God and each other. Thus, the conclusion of the biblical story of the flood raises a question that anticipates the emergence of Israel as a people enabled by Torah to resist the inclination toward evil and to become a blessing to humanity.

Overall observations

In the biblical story God accepts humans for what they are, establishing a covenant that promises humanity will not be destroyed again. The rainbow is the sign of that covenant, but the text makes it clear that this heavenly sign is as much for God as it is for people because it will serve as a reminder to the deity to not give in to the desire to destroy humanity again (Gen 9:8–17). There is an element of resignation in God's words in the biblical story that is not found in the Qur'an. The deity does not deny the presence of human sin and evil in the Islamic text, but places it within the wider framework of human goodness that is also present in the world.

In the Qur'an version, God wants human goodness to manifest itself and increase, whereas in the Bible this desire of God unfolds not in the Genesis flood story, but gradually in the subsequent narratives of the Pentateuch. In the biblical flood story, God is grieved and wishes to obliterate virtually all humans (and other animals) without a warning (Gen 6:5–13). After the flood things remain unchanged, and so God comes to terms with human evil initially by making a commitment that further destruction will not occur. Only later in the Pentateuch will God's main solution of choosing Israel emerge. The Qur'an version also anticipates its future founding leader, but it does so more explicitly, establishing Noah as a prophet who foreshadows Muhammad, as already discussed. Noah cautions his people, so that the flood is not a surprise as it is in the Bible. The people are given ample opportunity to mend their ways and turn their lives around, but they refuse to do so. In fact, their taunting becomes so belittling and demeaning that they are responsible for their own destruction: "Oh Noah, you have argued with us long and hard. Bring on us what you threaten us with, if you are among the truthful" (v. 32). The Qur'an's presentation of Noah as a warner, like Muhammad, has a significant bearing on the reader's impression of both his character and God's. The prophet is a spokesperson eager to help his people by telling them about a deity who wants to extend mercy to all.

Further Biblical Interpretations

Most of the biblical references to Noah or the flood story occur in the New Testament. Two of the prophetic books of the Hebrew Bible, Ezekiel and Isaiah, mention Noah. Ezekiel 14:12–20 presents a series of four hypothetical scenarios, each of which names Noah, Daniel, and Job as righteous individuals from the past. Each scenario imagines a land that God might punish in some way, and each ends by saying that if Noah, Daniel, and Job were in that land they would be able to save only themselves and no one else. The passage does not refer to the flood, but the second, third, and fourth scenarios add something that connects to it: "They would save neither son nor daughter; they would save only their own lives by their righteousness" (Ezek 14:20; cf. vv. 16, 18). The reference to their sons and daughters recalls the biblical flood story in which Noah's family is saved along with him; the Hebrew term used in Genesis for Noah's children (*bānêka*) could be read as sons only, or as all his children, including his daughters (Gen 6:18). This passage calls attention to Noah's outstanding reputation as an upright person that is highlighted at the beginning of the flood story (Gen 6:8; 7:1).

Ezekiel's theological interest in Noah, Daniel, and Job has simply to do with the righteousness of each, portraying them as heroes to make the point that the righteousness of each in the hypothetical situation would not benefit anyone but themselves. Ezekiel is addressed to Israelites in the wake of exile to Babylon and eventually the destruction of Jerusalem by the Babylonians. This passage makes clear, on the one hand, that not even the presence of a few righteous people could have prevented God from bringing about the destruction of Jerusalem. On the other hand, during and after the exile they were being told that God had allowed this catastrophe to occur as a punishment for how their ancestors had committed all manner of apostasy and social injustice. While such an explanation could serve to convey the importance of faithfulness to God and just living, it could also leave people feeling that they were suffering because of their ancestors and were themselves powerless. By linking each one's own behavior to their reward both here and in 18:21–23, Ezekiel seeks to energize his audience to right living that might lead to a better life.

There is a more direct reference to the flood in a section of the Book of Isaiah (chapters 40—55) that was written long after the eighth-century prophet Isaiah and that many scholars call "Second Isaiah." The reference occurs at the end of a passage in which God offers words of comfort and support to those who are oppressed or unhappy (Isa 54:1–10). In the first eight verses they are promised abundant offspring and told they will not suffer any shame because God is with them. The next verse makes a connection to Noah's time.

> ⁹This is like the days of Noah to me:
>   Just as I swore that the waters of Noah
>   would never again go over the earth,
> so I have sworn that I will not be angry with you
>   and will not rebuke you.
> ¹⁰For the mountains may depart
>   and the hills be removed,
> but my steadfast love shall not depart from you,
>   and my covenant of peace shall not be removed,
>   says the LORD, who has compassion on you. (Isa 54:9–10)

Scholars debate whether this passage was written during the exile in Babylon in the sixth century BCE or during the Persian period, but either way it would have addressed an audience enduring hardships. It seeks to encourage the people to remain faithful by reminding them that the covenant God established with them at the time of the flood continues in the midst of their difficulty. In this way, it interprets the Noah tradition to fit its own context. There is a possible further allusion to the flood in the next verse, where the audience is addressed in a way that could also describe the passengers in Noah's ark:

> O afflicted one, storm-tossed, and not comforted,
>   I am about to set your stones in antimony,
>   and lay your foundations with sapphires. (Isa 54:11).

In the New Testament, Noah appears in the Letter to the Hebrews. As discussed in chapter 3 regarding Cain and Abel, the eleventh chapter of Hebrews contains a lengthy composition that cites important figures from the past as models of faith, and one of them is Noah. "By faith Noah, warned by God about events as yet unseen, respected the warning and built an ark to save his household; by this he condemned the world and became an heir to the righteousness that is in accordance with faith" (Heb 11:7). The description of Noah here does not contain anything that directly contradicts or disagrees with the Genesis flood account, but a few verses later the author of Hebrews offers an interpretation of Noah and the other people from the past that introduces elements not found in the flood story.

> [13]All of these died in faith without having received the promises, but from a distance they saw and greeted them. They confessed that they were strangers and for-eigners on the earth, [14]for people who speak in this way make it clear that they are seeking a homeland. [15]If they had been thinking of the land that they had left behind, they would have had opportunity to return. [16]But as it is, they desire a better country, that is, a heavenly one. Therefore God is not ashamed to be called their God; indeed, he has prepared a city for them. (Heb 11:13–16)

These verses offer an interpretation of Noah and the others that is not supported by the account of the flood in Genesis 6—9. For the author of Hebrews, "promises" here refers mainly to what was promised to the patriarchs (Abraham, Isaac, and Jacob/Israel), but the text treats all the ancient characters together to make the point that what God promised to the ancestors in faith was ultimately fulfilled only in Christ. There is nothing explicit in that account about Noah seeing what was promised (Christ), but the author of Hebrews assumes that he could have seen it "from a distance" by faith. Similarly, Noah did not consider himself to be a stranger on the earth, nor was he able to return to the land he had left because it had been destroyed by the flood. In addition, the notion of a heavenly country is not mentioned in the flood story and it is not a concept present in the Hebrew Bible. This chapter of Hebrews has appropriated Noah and the other figures of the past to address a Christian audience, attempting to cultivate their faith in Jesus.

We find a more detailed Christian interpretation of the flood story in 1 Peter, a work probably written by a disciple of Peter in the last decade of the first century. "God waited patiently in the days of Noah, during the building of the ark, in which a few, that is, eight persons, were saved through water. And baptism, which this prefigured, now saves you—not as a removal of dirt from the body, but as an appeal to God for a good conscience, through the resurrection of Jesus Christ" (1 Pet 3:20–21). In this verse the number of people who entered the ark matches the Genesis account, where Noah, his wife, his three sons, and their wives are identified as those who were saved. However, the reference to God waiting patiently as the vessel was built is not found in the Genesis narrative. Beyond that, the primary interpretive move the author makes is in drawing a parallel between the flood and the waters of baptism, the ritual that marks initiation into faith in Jesus. The letter claims that just as Noah's family was saved through water so too are Christians who pass through the water of baptism.

The book that follows 1 Peter in the New Testament, 2 Peter, also contains a reference to Noah and the flood, but this time in support of the letter's view about what will happen in the end-time. Like 1 Peter, this work was not written by the disciple of that name, nor was it penned by the person who wrote 1 Peter. The author cites both Noah and Lot as people who remained righteous despite the sin and depravity of those around them, encouraging the audience to remain faithful until the end (2 Pet 2:5–10): "If [God] did not spare the ancient world, even though he saved Noah, a herald of righteousness, with seven others, when he brought a flood on a world of the ungodly…" (v. 5). Here too the number of survivors agrees with what is stated in Genesis, but there is evidence of interpretation in how Noah is presented. If meant to indicate that he was a proclaimer of some sort, the reference to him as a "herald of righteousness" is inaccurate in light of the fact that Noah does not utter a single word in the biblical account until after the flood has subsided. This description might be more appropriately applied to his role in the Qur'an, where Noah attempts to convince his people to abandon their sinful ways and follow God. The passage therefore raises the intriguing possibility that, by the time 2 Peter was written, Jewish or Christian traditions existed that interpreted Noah as a proclaimer/warner.

The flood story is also cited in the Gospels of Matthew and Luke in the context of a teaching by Jesus concerning the expectation of early Christians that he would return in the future.[11] Speaking about the last day Jesus says:

> [36]But about that day and hour no one knows, neither the angels of heaven, nor the Son, but only the Father. [37]For as the days of Noah were, so will be the coming of the Son of Man. [38]For as in those days before the flood they were eating and drinking, marrying and giving in marriage, until the day Noah entered the ark, [39]and they knew nothing until the flood came and swept them all away, so too will be the coming of the Son of Man. (Matt 24:36–39; cf. Luke 17:22–27)

This passage makes use of the flood story tradition to highlight the suddenness with which early Christians anticipated that Jesus would return and the world as they knew it would come to an end. Anticipating this would have helped them endure ongoing suffering despite their belief, based on their experience of the risen Jesus, that Jesus had defeated the power of death. Noah's contemporaries were caught unaware as they went about their daily lives, and to emphasize the unpredictability of the timing of Jesus's return would have encouraged faithful living day by day.

Focus for Comparison

By comparing the flood to the waters of baptism, 1 Peter puts forward an interpretation of the Noah story in Genesis that is similar to the one found in the Qur'an. Both texts are motivated by a desire to link Noah to a later figure of importance for their authors. With its reference to the salvific effect of Jesus's death and resurrection, this New Testament passage, like the passage from Hebrews discussed here, interprets the flood story through the lens of faith in Jesus as the savior who frees people from their sins (i.e., enables them to be in right relationship with God). The Qur'an puts words in Noah's mouth that he does not speak in the Bible in order to present him as a prophet, a proto-Muhammad who remains faithful to God even though his people reject the message he brings.

Questions to Consider

1. How significant is it that Noah speaks more frequently in the Qur'an than in Genesis?

2. Does it strike you as strange that a verse in the middle of the Qur'an's account of the flood (v. 35) is addressed to Muhammad?

3. Is the sin of association (*shirk*) similar to anything found in the Bible?

4. What is your reaction to how the Qur'an sometimes presents biblical figures in a way that attempts to support or legitimize Muhammad?

5. What do you find to be the most significant differences in how the Bible and the Qur'an tell the flood story?

6. What is your reaction to the idea of family as a religious category and not only a biological one?

7. What are your thoughts about how Noah and the flood story are interpreted in other parts of the Bible?

CHAPTER 5

Abraham and His Son

braham is a prominent figure in the Qur'an, and only Moses's name is mentioned more frequently in the text.[1] The Qur'an does not contain a lengthy narrative describing Abraham's life like the one in Genesis 11—25, but it highlights several scenes and themes that serve to present him as a monotheist who submitted himself to God. Some of this material is related to the biblical account and some is not. This chapter will focus mainly on how the story of Abraham's near sacrifice of his son is told in both the Bible and the Qur'an, while considering a few additional Qur'an passages in order to give a fuller sense of Abraham's role in Islam.

A passage in the third chapter of the Qur'an summarizes Islamic teaching on Abraham.

> [65]Oh, People of the Book! Why do you argue among yourselves about Abraham when the Torah and the Gospel were not revealed until after him? Will you not understand? [66]You are those who argued about that of which you had knowledge. Why do you argue about that of which you have no knowledge? God knows and you do not know. [67]Abraham was not a Jew or a Christian, but he was an upright person who submitted and was not one of those who associate. (Q 3:65–67)

These verses explain what Abraham was and what he was not. Because he predated the rise of both religions, he was neither a Jew nor a Christian. Its opening words indicate that this passage is directed to members of both those communities. The term "People of the Book" occurs many times in the Qur'an in reference to religions prior to Islam that received divine revelation in written form. In addition to Judaism and Christianity, Zoroastrianism is sometimes also included in this category.[2] In addition, the passage states that Abraham was not an idolater, and the Arabic word it uses (*mushrik*) describes someone who commits the sin of association (*shirk*).[3]

This passage rejects labels of "Jew," "Christian," and "idolater" for Abraham, while bestowing two others on him: *hanif* (*ḥanīf*), translated "upright person"; and *muslim*, translated "one who submitted." "Hanif" occurs twelve times in the Qur'an, and Abraham is the only person identified as a hanif. Outside the Qur'an the term describes someone who inclines toward a proper state or way of life, and here it has the sense of someone with a pure monotheistic faith. Eleven of the twelve occurrences of "hanif" in the Qur'an are immediately followed by a word (*mushrik*) that is its antithesis. The point being made in this passage is that Abraham personifies the true believer and in no way can he be associated with idolatry, the worst sin a person can commit. The other Arabic term used for Abraham is "muslim." The Qur'an identifies a number of biblical figures as "muslims," which should not be confused with "Muslims." The capitalized spelling refers to those who follow the religion that traces its origin to the Prophet Muhammad in seventh-century Arabia. The lowercase spelling has a less specific sense, describing those who submit themselves to God without necessarily embracing Islam. When the Qur'an refers to Abraham and other figures from the past as muslims, it highlights the connection between the message of Muhammad and that of other prophets who came before him.

The Qur'an identifies both Isaac and Ishmael as Abraham's sons and considers them, like their father, to be prophets. Other than a passage featuring Ishmael that anticipates construction of the Islamic shrine at Mecca (Q 2:125–29; discussed below), the Qur'an hardly ever shows Abraham in the company of one of his sons. Another example of such a pairing appears in the passage that describes how Abraham almost killed one of his sons, but there is an interesting issue surrounding that text—we do not know which son almost lost his life. The lack of a name for the intended victim is not the only significant difference between the Qur'an's version of the scene and the one described in Genesis 22:1–19.

The Near Sacrifice of Abraham's Son

[100][Abraham prayed,] "My Lord, grant me one from among the righteous." [101]So We gave him the good news of a mild-mannered son. [102]When he was old enough to work with him he said, "Oh my son, I have dreamed that I should sacrifice you. What do you think of that?" He said, "Oh my father, do what you have been commanded. If God wills, you will find me patient." [103]When they both submitted and he threw him face down, [104]We called to him, "Oh Abraham, [105]You have fulfilled the dream." Thus do We reward those who do good. [106]Truly, that was a clear test, [107]and We ransomed him with a great sacrifice. [108]Through the succeeding generations We left upon him the salutation: [109]"Peace be upon Abraham!" [110]Thus do We reward those who do good. [111]Truly, he was among our believing servants. [112]And We gave him the good news of Isaac, a prophet from among the righteous.

COMPARISON WITH THE BIBLICAL NARRATIVE

The two versions of the near sacrifice share these four main points in common:

1. A reference is made to God testing Abraham. (Gen 22:1; Q 37:106)
2. Abraham lays his son down to sacrifice him. (Gen 22:9; Q 37:103)
3. A voice calls out and stops Abraham from sacrificing his son. (Gen 22:11–12; Q 37:104)

4. God blesses Abraham and his offspring. (Gen 22:17–18; Q 37:113)

The ransom and sacrifice mentioned in verse 107 of the Qur'an passage could be connected to the scene in the Bible in which Abraham sacrifices a ram in place of Isaac (Gen 22:13), but since the nature of the sacrifice is not specified in the Qur'an, it has not been included in this list of similarities. Consequently, only four of the Qur'an's fourteen verses and six of the Bible's nineteen verses have a direct connection with the other text.

INTERPRETATION OF ABRAHAM

This well-known biblical scene has been discussed and represented by theologians, philosophers, ethicists, and artists through the ages.[4] One quality of the Genesis account that makes it so memorable is the way it draws readers in and forces them to consider what happens in the story from the perspectives of both Abraham and Isaac. The fact that the characters' thoughts and reactions are never revealed endows the narrative with an element of mystery and uncertainty.

As is typical when it relates traditions found in the Bible, the Qur'an does not contain much narrative detail. There is no information on where the near sacrifice took place, whether Abraham and his son had to travel to get there, or on cutting the wood, loading the donkey, or wielding the knife. The most significant narrative gap involves the identity of the son, and Muslim commentators have discussed this question throughout history. Early on, there was a tendency to see Isaac as the intended victim, but over time that opinion shifted such that the dominant view today sees Ishmael as the one who was almost sacrificed by Abraham. Isaac is mentioned by name in verse 112, but this does not clear up the uncertainty over which son was nearly killed. The end of the passage states that Abraham was given the good news of Isaac (v. 112), but the relationship of this statement to the story that has just been told is unclear. If the passage is read sequentially so that Abraham is told of Isaac's birth after the near sacrifice, then Ishmael was the one who almost lost his life. But if verse 112 is meant to summarize the story, then perhaps it was Isaac. A point in favor of the latter alternative is the fact that the word "righteous" (*ṣāliḥ*) that describes Isaac in verse 112 is the same one that Abraham uses in verse 100 to refer to the son who is nearly put to death, but this repeated word does not definitively tip the scales in favor of Isaac.

The anonymity of the son in the Qur'an suggests that his identity is not important for the story or the lesson it imparts. The son's lack of a name might be intended to portray him as a symbolic figure who represents a type of person rather than as a specific individual like Ishmael or Isaac. We have seen such narrative purpose in the chapter on Cain and Abel, which discussed how Adam's two sons are unnamed in the Qur'an and personify two different types of people. The point of the Qur'an's version of the Abraham story is that Abraham nearly sacrificed one of his sons, not the identity of the one he almost killed.

The son's name remains unknown in the Qur'an, but something else about him is revealed—he is old enough to work with Abraham (v. 102). The Arabic root of the word that describes this quality (*saʿā*) can mean "to be active or busy" and "to engage in an activity with energy," and this suggests that Abraham's son has reached an age that allows him to be of physical assistance to his father. Another well-attested meaning of the root relates to one's mental and moral capacity and might be translated "to behave in conformity with one's judgment." If this sense is applied to the Qur'an passage, then it is saying that Abraham's son has reached the age of reason, is able to think for himself and act accordingly.

This is the very quality the son demonstrates when Abraham asks him what is undoubtedly one of the strangest questions in the Qur'an (v. 102a): "Oh my son, I have dreamed that I should sacrifice you. What do you think of that?" The son's response is immediate and unambiguous, and it expresses his submission to the divine will (v. 102b). The son encourages Abraham to do as he has been instructed, and he informs his father that with God's help he will be able to accept it. The next words in the passage contain the Arabic verb (*aslam*) from which the word "Islam" is derived, and they describe a joint surrender on the part of father and son as they both submit to God. Without using the exact word, the passage presents Abraham and his son as Muslims.

The biblical account uses a different term to describe the son when God refers to him as "your son, your only son Isaac, whom you love" (Gen 22:2). The adjective "only" is significant because of Isaac's role as the one who will carry on the covenant that God has made with Abraham and his offspring forever (Gen 17:19). The order to sacrifice Isaac puts that future at risk, and his designation as Abraham's only son underscores the radical trust that God is demanding of Abraham. The Qur'an refers to God's covenant with Israel in places, but it is not a significant part of its presentation of Abraham, which makes sense because Abraham is a universal figure in Islam, identified in the passage above as a hanif ("upright person") and neither a Jew nor a Christian. The biblical concept of covenant is tied to the idea that Israel is God's chosen people. This does not align with the Islamic view that God is the God of all people, and so the concept of covenant does not play a prominent role in the Qur'an.

While most interpretations of the Genesis story tend to focus on Abraham's faith, the story in the Qur'an is as much about the son's faith as it is about the father's. In fact, it could be said that in the Islamic text Abraham's faith is dependent upon his son's. It is unclear what motivates Abraham to ask his son what he thinks about the dream that he has had, but given its content he is likely deeply troubled by the dream. He turns to his son in an attempt to make sense of it. Without hesitation the son tells his father that he must do as he has been instructed and, with God's assistance, he himself will not be an obstacle to his father's ability to carry it out. It is that self-surrender on his son's part that then allows Abraham to make a similar leap of faith and enable them to both submit. Both versions of the episode refer to it as a test, but who is being tested? The account in Genesis leaves little doubt as it opens with the statement, "After these things God tested Abraham" (Gen 22:1a). But the placement and ambiguity of the testing theme in the Qur'an suggest that it is not only Abraham who is on trial, but his son as well. The Islamic text introduces the theme not at the outset of the passage, but only after both the father and the son have submitted (v. 106).

The role that the son plays as a catalyst for his father in the Qur'an highlights a similar dynamic present in the biblical version. Genesis 22 does not provide any information on Isaac other than the reference to him being Abraham's "only" son. It does not say anything about his age like the Islamic text does, but Isaac cannot be very young because his father has him carry the firewood for the sacrifice (Gen 22:6). The critical moment in the Qur'an passage is Abraham's question to his son, the answer to which makes possible the submission of both characters. Similarly, Genesis also reports only one exchange between the father and the son, but in this case it is Isaac who asks the key question. "Isaac said to his father Abraham, 'Father!' And he said, 'Here I am, my son.' He said, 'The fire and the wood are here, but where is the lamb for a burnt offering?' Abraham said, 'God himself will provide the lamb for a burnt offering, my son.' So the two of them walked on together" (Gen 22:7–8). With this question, the biblical son shows an ability to size up and evaluate his circumstances like his Islamic counterpart does. Just as in the Qur'an, the son's words lead the father to respond in a manner that expresses his faith and confidence in God. It is therefore a striking similarity that both texts report a question and answer as the only meaningful dialogue that takes place between Abraham and his son, and in both cases that brief conversation leads to an expression of faith on Abraham's part. In this respect the Qur'an retains a significant element of the Genesis account, and the way the Islamic text presents the story illuminates an aspect of the biblical tradition.

Muhammad's Forerunner

The Qur'an interprets the figure of Abraham also by highlighting his role as a hanif who rejects polytheism and promotes monotheism. Some passages describe him urging his contemporaries to put aside false worship, and others explain how he instituted a religious system centered on following the one God. These texts describe scenes that are not in the Bible, but some of them have parallels in extrabiblical Jewish texts. Beyond putting forward a particular understanding of Abraham the hanif, these Qur'an passages also indirectly refer to the prophet of Islam because they sometimes mirror, anticipate, and even predict some of the events and circumstances of Muhammad's life.

ABRAHAM, THE CRITIC OF POLYTHEISM

[41]Mention Abraham in the book. Truly, he was trustworthy and a prophet. [42]He said to his father, "Oh my

father, why do you worship what does not hear, does not see, and cannot help you in anything? ⁴³Oh my father, knowledge has come to me that has not come to you. So follow me and I will guide you on a proper path. ⁴⁴Oh my father, do not worship Satan. Truly, Satan is disobedient to the merciful One. ⁴⁵Oh my father, I fear that a punishment from the merciful One will come upon you and you will become a friend of Satan." ⁴⁶He said, "Are you forsaking my gods, oh Abraham? If you do not stop this, I will stone you. Leave my presence!" ⁴⁷Abraham said, "Peace be upon you. I will ask forgiveness from my Lord for you. Truly, He is kind to me. ⁴⁸I will separate myself from you and from what you call upon that is not God, and I will call upon my Lord. Perhaps in calling upon my Lord I will not be in distress." ⁴⁹When he separated himself from them and from what they worshipped that was not God We gave to him Isaac and Jacob, and We made each of them a prophet. ⁵⁰And We gave to them of Our mercies and granted them true and high renown. (Q 19:41–50)

This is one of multiple passages in the Qur'an that describe how Abraham attempted to convince his people to reject polytheism (cf. Q 6:74–83; 21:51–71; 26:69–86; 29:16–27; 37:83–98; 43:26–27; 60:4). They sometimes show him destroying their idols, and in some, Abraham's father plays a role, as in this one. This passage reports the lengthiest conversation between the two in the Qur'an, and it graphically portrays the tension and conflict between father and son. Abraham attempts to appeal to their biological relationship, as he uses the term "father" four times (vv. 42–45) and reminds him of the danger and punishment that result from following Satan. But the older man avoids calling Abraham his son and threatens to kill him if he does not leave him alone. Abraham obeys his father and leaves his presence, but before doing so assures him that he will continue to ask God to forgive him and his people.

This story would have struck a nerve in Muhammad and the early Muslim community. According to Islamic sources, since the Prophet's parents died when he was young, he would not have experienced a radical and dramatic break with them like the one described in this passage. But later in his life—particularly early in his career—his message was not well received, and so he was not a stranger to tense relationships and rejection. Things got so bad for him and his followers in Mecca that when the invitation to move to Yathrib (later known as Medina) came their way in 622, they jumped at the opportunity to relocate there rather than run the risk of further alienation and possible physical harm from their Meccan neighbors. The description of Abraham's departure (vv. 48–49) can be viewed as a migration (*hijrah*) similar to the one the first Muslims took when they made the trek from Mecca to Medina. Both Abraham and Muhammad experienced rejection and were forced to flee when people close to them refused to accept their monotheistic messages. Knowing that this same experience was shared by Abraham and the other prior prophets would have been a source of comfort and support for Muhammad and his early followers.

This passage has some connection to legends about Abraham found in extrabiblical Jewish writings. The Apocalypse of Abraham, from the first or second century CE, explains how Abraham tried to persuade his father to give up the worship of idols, but his father refused and became angry at Abraham. A similar exchange is recorded in the book of Jubilees, where Abraham's father agrees with his son about the powerlessness of idols but continues to pretend to believe in them for his own safety and survival (Jub. 12:1–7).[5]

ABRAHAM, THE CHAMPION OF MONOTHEISM

Nowhere does the Qur'an establish a closer link between Abraham and Muhammad than in chapter 2 (vv. 125–29). Whereas the passage in the section just discussed describes the way Abraham attempted to root out polytheism within his family and among his people, this one explains how he literally laid the foundation upon which Islam would be established centuries later.

[125]We made the house a sanctuary and security for the people. Take the place of Abraham as a place of prayer.

> We commanded Abraham and Ishmael to purify My house for those who walk around it, the devout, and those who bow and prostrate. [126]Abraham said, "Lord, make this land secure and provide fruit to its inhabitants who believe in God and the last day." God said, "I will make the unbelievers prosper for a while and then I will lead them to punishment of fire. How wretched will that fate be." [127]Abraham and Ishmael raised the foundations of the house saying, "Our Lord, accept it from us. You are the all-hearing One, the all-knowing One. [128]Our Lord, make us submissive to You, and make of our offspring a community submissive to You. Show us our forms of worship, and mercifully turn to us for You are the often-returning One, the merciful One. [129]Our Lord, send to them a messenger from among them who will recite Your revelations to them and teach them the book and wisdom so that he may purify them. You are truly the mighty One, the wise One." (Q 2:125–29)

Here Abraham and his son Ishmael build the "House of God," which is a reference to the Kaaba (ka'bah) located in the center of the Grand Mosque of Mecca in modern-day Saudi Arabia. This cube-shaped building that is usually covered with a black embroidered cloth is the focal point for Muslims all over the world who turn to face it during the five times a day they pray. The present structure, although relatively recent, is built on a site that has been a place of pilgrimage and prayer for centuries. According to this passage, the Kaaba was originally constructed by Muhammad's prophetic forebears Abraham and Ishmael. It had become a center of polytheistic worship for a long time prior to Muhammad's prophetic career, but he restored it to its monotheistic origin in the decade prior to his death in 632.

Its Abrahamic roots are apparent to anyone who enters the Kaaba today because there is a small building near it that contains the impression of two feet and is referred to as the "place of Abraham" (maqām Ibrahīm) that is mentioned in verse 125. Several other elements of this passage relate directly to Islamic beliefs and practices. The reference to those who walk around the House of God (v. 125) describes an important Islamic ritual that takes place at the Kaaba. Making the pilgrimage to Mecca is one of the five pillars of Islamic practice that Muslims are expected to engage in as expressions of their membership in the community.[6] Those who can afford to do it and are physically able to travel should at some point in their lives journey to Mecca to perform the rituals associated with the pilgrimage, which takes place during the twelfth month of the Muslim calendar. The pilgrimage comprises a set of prescribed activities that take place over a week's time during the first half of the month. One of those rituals entails processing around the Kaaba seven times in a counterclockwise direction. Muslims also circumambulate the Kaaba throughout the rest of the year, but do not do so during prayer times. The words to Abraham in this passage about those who walk around the House of God are therefore an allusion to one of the key ways that Muslims demonstrate their faith.

That is also the case with the mention of "those who bow and prostrate" in the same verse. These movements are two of the essential elements of Muslim prayer, and both are done repeatedly during the five daily prayer times. With these references to pilgrimage and prayer, the passage associates Abraham with two of the five pillars of Islam, and it identifies him as the person responsible for building the structure that will become the geographic center of the religion of Islam centuries later.

Once they have constructed the House of God, Abraham and Ishmael offer up a prayer that also establishes a link between themselves and the Muslim community. They first ask God to bless them and those who will come after them (v. 128). The two words in the first sentence that are translated "submissive" come from the same root as do "Islam" and "Muslim." Abraham and Ishmael pray that God will help them and those in future generations to be submissive to the divine will, and the choice of vocabulary underscores the connection between their faith and that of Muslims in the future. Their next words further highlight that connection, as they ask God to send a messenger "from among them" (v. 129). Abraham's role as a precursor to Muhammad could not be any clearer. He and his son Ishmael are at the Kaaba in Mecca asking God to send to their offspring a messenger who will bring them divine revelation. That messenger, of course, will be Muhammad, and the revelation will be the Qur'an.

Further Biblical Interpretations

There are approximately a dozen references to Abraham outside Genesis 12—25 in the Hebrew Bible, but most of them are found in formulaic expressions like "the God of Abraham, Isaac, and Jacob." One strikingly different passage in the Book of Isaiah employs unusual imagery to describe Abraham and Sarah:

> Listen to me, you that pursue righteousness,
>   you that seek the LORD.
> Look to the rock from which you were hewn,
>   and to the quarry from which you were dug.
> Look to Abraham your father
>   and to Sarah who bore you;
> for he was but one when I called him,
>   but I blessed him and made him many. (Isa 51:1–2)

The passage refers to Abraham and Sarah as a rock and a quarry, suggesting that they are the foundation or source of the Israelite community living in difficult circumstances to whom the text is addressed.[7] They are the Israelites' ancestors, and the reference to God blessing Abraham and giving him many offspring recalls the initial promise God made to Abraham in Genesis 12:1–3. Referring to Abraham and Sarah as a rock and a quarry conveys a sense of durability and permanence to express the idea that Abraham's descendants will endure forever.

The New Testament contains multiple references to Abraham and his family, whose lives are interpreted in ways that support an author's Christian message. Of the Gospels, Matthew begins by describing Jesus as the "son of David, the son of Abraham" (1:1). There follows a genealogy of Jesus that lists Abraham as the first of his ancestors. By presenting Jesus's lineage in this way, Matthew conveys to his Jewish audience that Jesus continues the story of salvation begun with God's promise to Abraham and continued through David. Luke is the only Gospel that contains a parable of Jesus in which Abraham plays a role (16:19–34), and it records the only words Abraham speaks in the Bible outside the Book of Genesis. Jesus tells a story about an unnamed rich man and a poor man named Lazarus who both die, with the rich man going to hell while Lazarus goes to heaven, where he is in the company of Abraham.[8] The rich man calls out to Abraham to ask him to send Lazarus back to earth so he can warn the man's brothers to live better lives and so avoid the punishment he is now experiencing. He pleads with Abraham that his brothers will certainly listen to someone who has come back from the dead, but Abraham disagrees and says that if they are not already obeying Moses and the prophets, they will not care if someone returns from the dead. In this parable Abraham supports Jesus's teaching concerning how riches can separate one from God (Luke 6:20, 24; 18:25). Moreover, by mentioning one who returns from the dead, Luke alludes to Jesus and so allows Abraham to anticipate and critique the refusal of some people to accept that Jesus rose from the dead.

On the issue of works and faith, references to Abraham in the fourth chapter of Paul's Letter to the Romans and in the Letter of James may seem to support opposite claims, but the two texts use the term *works* differently and so are not in conflict. Paul expresses two concerns here: one broader and one more specific. Broadly speaking, Paul emphasizes that God bestows salvation in Christ to people without their having to earn it; they simply need to receive it in faith. More specifically, Paul was concerned to convince his Jewish Christian audience that to become Christians, Gentiles need not follow Jewish laws, including circumcision and dietary laws; he believed that doing such "works" of the Jewish law was an unnecessary burden to place on Gentiles who come to faith in Christ. In Romans he cites Abraham as a model of true faith who was deemed righteous even before he was circumcised: "For what does the scripture say? 'Abraham believed God, and it was reckoned to him as righteousness'" (Rom 4:3). Here Paul is citing Genesis 15:6, and at that point in the Genesis narrative, Abraham, who has already put faith into action by leaving his home and going where God commanded, is now asked to trust that God will provide descendants to him and Sarah, who remain childless in their old age. Abraham has not yet, however, received the command to be circumcised. Directing his audience, which included Jewish Christians, to the Genesis passage, Paul equates Abraham's faith with faith in Jesus and his resurrection: "Now the words, 'it was reckoned to him,' were written not for his sake alone, but for ours also. It will be reckoned to us who believe in him who raised Jesus our Lord from the dead, who was handed over to death for our trespasses and was raised for our justification" (Rom 4:23–25). In this way, Abraham's faith becomes an example for all Christians to emulate and supports Paul's insistence that faith in Christ does not require Gentiles to observe Jewish laws.

The author of the Letter of James understands "works" broadly as actions that express faith concretely (cf. Jas 1:19–27; 2:14–26). Paul would not dispute the idea that faith in Christ expresses itself in tangible ways, as attested by Paul's own example of generous service. To illustrate the importance of expressing faith through action, the author of James cites Abraham's near sacrifice of Isaac as an example.

> [21]Was not our ancestor Abraham justified by works when he offered his son Isaac on the altar? [22]You see that faith was active along with his works, and faith was brought to completion by the works. [23]Thus the scripture was fulfilled that says, "Abraham believed God, and it was reckoned to him as righteousness," and he was called the friend of God. [24]You see that a person is justified by works and not by faith alone. (Jas 2:21–24)

As Paul does in Romans 4, this author also quotes Genesis 15:6, but does so by creatively linking the affirmation of Abraham's faith in that part of the story to Abraham's faith expressed in obedient willingness to sacrifice Isaac in Genesis 22. In Genesis 15, however, Abraham's belief is a response to God's telling him that his descendants will outnumber the stars; it does not involve Abraham putting his faith into action and so does not support the author's view of the necessity of expressing faith through works. To convey that idea, the author creatively links the commendation of Abraham's faith from Genesis 15 with Abraham's willingness to enact his belief by obediently sacrificing Isaac in Genesis 22, where divine affirmation comes via an angel in different words: "I know that you fear God, since you have not withheld your son, your only son, from me" (Gen 22:12b). The description of Abraham as the friend of God in the Letter of James is interesting because this same title is given to Abraham in both the Hebrew Bible (Isa 41:8; 2 Chr 20:7) and the Qur'an (Q 4:125).

Focus for Comparison

In their interpretations of Abrahamic traditions, the New Testament and the Qur'an employ similar arguments to make a case for his relevance, portraying Abraham as the ancestor to whom Christians and Muslims, respectively, trace their roots. Some New Testament writings attempt to link Abraham with Jesus, as seen, for example, in the genealogy in Matthew. In the Qur'an, Abraham anticipates the coming of Muhammad as he and Ishmael pray to God for the coming of the future prophet of Islam. Paul's claim in Romans 4 that Abraham predated the law supports his argument for accepting Gentiles into Christianity without requiring them to obey the Jewish laws. The Qur'an asserts that Abraham was a person of faith even though he was neither a Jew nor a Christian; it presents Abraham as establishing central Islamic practices of pilgrimage to and worship at Mecca, practices to which all humanity is invited.

Questions to Consider

1. Is Abraham a unifying figure for Jews, Christians, and Muslims? Explain.

2. What is your reaction to how the Qur'an refers to Abraham and other figures of the past as "muslims"?

3. How does the lack of a name for the son whom Abraham almost sacrifices have an impact on the Qur'an story?

4. Beyond the lack of the son's name, what are other key differences between how the Qur'an and the Bible relate the tradition about Abraham's near sacrifice?

5. Do you think connecting him with Abraham is an effective way for the Qur'an to legitimate the prophetic status of Muhammad?

6. How might we explain the fact that the Qur'an mentions things about Abraham that are sometimes found in extrabiblical Jewish sources?

7. What is your reaction to the way other biblical passages interpret Abraham?

CHAPTER 6

Moses and the Golden Calf

Moses is the most frequently mentioned individual in the Qur'an. A succinct summary of his role in Islam appears in chapter 19: "Remember Moses in the book. Truly, he was a chosen one, a messenger, a prophet. We called him from the right side of the mountain and drew him near in communion. We gave him, out of Our mercy, his brother Aaron, a prophet" (vv. 51–53). This passage gives Moses two important titles: messenger (*rasūl*) and prophet (*nabī*). In the Qur'an the difference between these two roles is not completely clear. All people identified in the text as messengers are also considered to be prophets, but not all prophets are messengers. The most prominent individuals who are given both titles are Moses, Jesus, and Muhammad. The Qur'an also portrays each of these three as having been given revelation in the form of a book that he delivered to his people—Moses was given the Torah, Jesus the gospel, and Muhammad the Qur'an. Moses's identity as a messenger and prophet who was given a book closely aligns him with Muhammad (Q 3:3). Here we will consider how the Qur'an presents and interprets a couple of well-known traditions related to Moses—his birth and the story of the golden calf.[1]

Moses's Birth Story

The story of Moses's mother placing her infant son in a basket on the river to save him is one of the most well-known in the Bible, and the Qur'an's version of the events is similar to it in many ways. As is the case with all stories the two texts share, though, the Islamic one puts its own unique spin on it.

[3] We relate to you in truth a story of Moses and Pharaoh for a people who believe. [4] Truly, Pharaoh was master over the land and divided its people into different groups. He weakened one group of them by slaying their sons and allowing their women to live. Truly, he was one of the evildoers. [5] We wished to show favor to those who were weakened in the land, to make them leaders and heirs [6] and to establish them in the land to make Pharaoh, Haman, and their legions see from them that which they feared. [7] We announced to Moses' mother, "Suckle him, and if you fear for him toss him into the river. Do not fear or grieve, for We will restore him to you and make him one of the messengers." [8] Pharaoh's family picked him up and he became an enemy and cause of sorrow for them. Truly, Pharaoh, Haman, and their legions were sinners. [9] Pharaoh's wife said, "He will be a joy for me and for you. Do not kill him. Perhaps he will be of some use to us or we may take him as a son." They were not aware [of what was going to happen]. [10] Moses' mother became anxious and she was about to reveal it, had We not strengthened her heart in order that she might be a believer. [11] She said to his sister, "Follow him!" So she watched him from a distance and they were unaware. [12] We had already caused him to refuse the wet nurses so she said, "Shall I direct you to a household that will raise him for you and take care of him?" [13] Thus We returned him to his mother so that she might have joy and not grieve and in order that she might know that God's promise is true, although most do not know.

96

COMPARISON WITH THE BIBLICAL NARRATIVE

The same narrative outline is found in both this passage and the account of Moses's birth in Exodus 1—2. The characters all play the same roles in both texts, and their similar actions result in the same outcome. Beneath that commonality, though, the events take on unique significance in the Qur'an because of the way it interprets the biblical story.

1. The Egyptian ruler calls for the deaths of Hebrew male babies. (Exod 1:15–22; Q 28:4).
2. Moses's mother saves him by placing him on the river. (Exod 2:3; Q 28:7).
3. The child is found by a member of the Pharaoh's family. (Exod 2:5–6; Q 28:8–9).
4. Moses's sister is involved in returning the child to his mother. (Exod 2:7–9; Q 28:11–13).

Of the elements in the qur'anic version that are not in the biblical one, several do not have a significant impact on the meaning of the passage. For example, in Exodus it is the Pharaoh's daughter who finds the infant in the river, but in the Qur'an his wife is the family member who plays a key role. Similarly, the Qur'an does not state that Moses's mother returns him to Pharaoh's family after he is weaned, as is reported in the Bible (Exod 2:10a). Moreover, the Qur'an twice mentions someone named Haman (vv. 6, 8), who is not found in Exodus. In both verses Pharaoh, Haman, and their troops are mentioned, and so perhaps Haman is a military advisor or counselor to the Egyptian ruler. He and Pharaoh are mentioned in four other places in the Qur'an (28:38; 29:39–40; 40:23–24, 36–37). In the Bible a man named Haman is a character in the Book of Esther (3:1–6; 7:6–10), where he is a minister of the Persian ruler and an enemy of the Jewish people. While non-Muslim scholars have at times proposed a connection between the Haman of Esther and the one in the Qur'an, this suggestion has not been accepted by most Muslim commentators. Some Muslim scholars maintain that Haman is not a personal name but a title referring to the high priest of the Egyptian god Amon.

INTERPRETATION OF MOSES'S BIRTH

One character mentioned in the Qur'an's version of the events but not in the biblical one has great interpretive significance—God. At key junctures in the story the deity plays a critical role by influencing the behavior and thoughts of the characters. While details of the larger Exodus narrative may imply that God is acting "behind the scenes" in this story, God's activity is not explicit, nor is God even mentioned. The Qur'an actually attributes the plan for how to save the child to God, who instructs Moses's mother to feed the child and place him on the river (v. 7), and to display faith in God by going against her parental instincts and abandoning her newborn son, trusting that she will be reunited with him. The absence of a basket or container for the child in the passage further underscores her degree of faith. By having God call Moses a messenger (v. 7), the Qur'an further interprets the tradition by giving him a title held by very few that signals the important place the child will hold in human history.

Moses's mother faithfully follows God's instructions but soon begins to waver, and once again the deity intervenes to make sure the child will be safe (v. 10). The verb (*rabaṭa*) that describes God's action in this verse means "to tie up," and its three occurrences in the Qur'an all take someone's heart as the object (Q 8:11; 18:14). Here, the mother feels anxiety over the loss of her son, and the deity responds by binding and tightening up her heart to give her the resolve she needs to not give in to her despair.

The mother is not the only character in the story whose behavior is influenced by God. In a display of divine control over basic human instinct, the deity causes the baby to reject the breasts that would feed him, and this is what allows the mother and child to be reunited (v. 12a). Through this triple intervention in the story—commanding the mother to place the child in the river, strengthening her heart, and controlling the infant's eating habits—God steps in at key moments to influence the outcome.

The Golden Calf Story

The Bible and the Qur'an both describe an incident involving the Israelites that began while Moses was on a mountain receiving

98

the tablets of the law from God. They tell how the people went astray in violation of the command to worship only God by creating and worshiping an idol in the form of a golden calf. While the Qur'an contains an additional version of the golden calf episode in chapter 20 (vv. 86–98), we will focus on the version in chapter 7 (vv. 148–54).

> [148]During Moses' absence his people made from their ornaments a calf that made a lowing sound. Did they not see that it did not speak to them and it did not guide them? They took it [for worship] and were transgressors. [149]When they repented and realized they had gone astray they said, "If our Lord will not have mercy on us and forgive us our sins, we will surely be among the lost ones." [150]When Moses, angry and grieving, returned to his people he said, "What you have done in my absence is evil! Are you so quick to bring on your Lord's judgement?" He threw down the tablets and grabbed his brother by the hair, pulling him toward himself. His brother said, "Son of my mother, the people overtook me and were about to kill me. Do not let the enemies rejoice over my misfortune and do not include me among the transgressors." [151]Moses said, "My Lord, forgive me and my brother and bring us into Your mercy, You who are the most merciful of all." [152]Anger from their Lord and humiliation in the present life will come to those who took the calf. Thus do We reward those who invent falsehood. [153]But for those who do evil and then repent and believe, truly your Lord is forgiving and merciful after that. [154]When Moses' anger had subsided, he took the tablets. In their writing is guidance and mercy for those who fear their Lord.

COMPARISON WITH THE
BIBLICAL NARRATIVE

As is the case in the narrative surrounding Moses's birth, the general outline of the golden calf narrative is quite similar in the

Bible and the Qur'an, as demonstrated by a comparison of shared elements.

1. Moses's absence is described. (Q 7:148; Exod 32:1)
2. The calf is made from jewelry. (Q 7:148; Exod 32:2–3)
3. The people worship the calf. (Q 7:148; Exod 32:5–6)
4. Moses is angry when he returns, and he throws down the tablets. (Q 7:150; Exod 32:19)
5. Moses confronts Aaron. (Q 7:150; Exod 32:21–24)
6. Moses asks God's forgiveness. (Q 7:151–52a; Exod 32:30–32; 33:12–13, 15–16; 34:9)
7. God responds to Moses's request. (Q 7:152b–53; Exod 32:33—33:5; 33:14, 17; 34:6–7)

However, the two stories and their messages diverge in significant ways. The Qur'an's version is much more concise than the biblical account and corresponds mainly to elements in Exodus 32, while the biblical story continues in Exodus 33—34. In Exodus, a series of dialogues between God and Moses include working out a reconciliation over whether God will continue to punish the Israelites by refusing to accompany them on their wilderness journey; God relents and agrees to accompany them (Exod 32:34—33:6; 33:12–17). In Exodus, Moses breaks the tablets when throwing them down in anger. In the Qur'an, since Moses throws them but does not break them, there is no need for a second set. A concluding scene in Exodus describes the creation of replacement tablets and an appearance by God to Moses (Exod 33:18—34:9), in which God solemnly declares,

> The Lord, the Lord,
> a God merciful and gracious,
> slow to anger,
> and abounding in steadfast love and faithfulness,
> keeping steadfast love for the thousandth generation,
> forgiving iniquity and transgression and sin,
> yet by no means clearing the guilty,
> but visiting the iniquity of the parents

upon the children
and the children's children,
to the third and the fourth generation. (34:6–7)[2]

Here, "merciful" translates the Hebrew term *raḥûm*, which is cognate to the Arabic term *raḥima* "to have mercy" that the Qur'an attributes to God.

INTERPRETATION OF THE GOLDEN CALF STORY

Recognizing that both Exodus and the Qur'an are interpreting prior traditions for their own purposes in telling the story of the golden calf is especially helpful for understanding the differences and similarities between them. While the account in Exodus 32—34 emphasizes the people's sin and punishment before shifting to reconciliation and God's mercy, the relatively concise Islamic text moves quickly from a brief mention of sin to an emphasis on God's mercy. In both stories, God demonstrates mercy and forgiveness. In the Exodus story, however, these qualities emerge only as part of a difficult process that also involves severe punishment. After explaining how the story's emphasis on punishment would have helped the Israelite audience of Exodus survive their historical situation, the following discussion unfolds by focusing on each of the main characters in the story: the Israelites, Aaron, Moses, and God.

To understand the emphasis in Exodus on both the Israelites' offense against God and the painful process of punishment that precedes reconciliation, it is helpful to consider the historical situation to which this text was responding.[3] If we are to imagine the stories told in Exodus as occurring during a historical period, it would be the thirteenth century BCE. However, it is important for interpreting these stories to recognize that they were written centuries after that. Exodus was likely edited into its final (or nearly final) form during the sixth century BCE, after the Babylonians had destroyed Jerusalem and taken many Israelites into exile in Babylon. In the wake of prior devastations of Northern Israel by the Assyrians more than a century prior, these catastrophic events left Israel on the brink of extinction, and were interpreted by multiple biblical writers as a punishment brought on the people by many generations of violations of their covenant with God, especially through social injustices and the worship of gods other than the God of Israel. Recent scholarship explains how such interpretations with their violent divine images would have helped people traumatized by those events to survive.[4] Exodus 32—34 does not explicitly mention those catastrophic events, but the parallels would have been clear to the ancient audience. These chapters describe how Israel's ancestors in faith sinned gravely and endured horrific punishment that threatened to wipe them out—but did not; the punishment was instead followed by reconciliation with God and an affirmation of God's mercy. By telling the story in this way, the writers offered their beleaguered sixth-century audience both solidarity in their present suffering and a foundation for trusting in God's desire to be reconciled with them and show them mercy. It is likely that centuries prior, in a brief version of the story, the calf was considered a legitimate symbol of Israel's God, so that there was no sin. Eventually, calf images of Israel's God were prohibited, and the story told in Exodus reflects that change. The inclusion of sin in the story, followed by reconciliation and the promise of divine mercy, allowed Israelites after the destruction of Jerusalem and exile to see their own suffering and desire for God's mercy reflected both in the words and actions of their ancestors and in God's response.

The Israelites

In both the Bible and the Qur'an, the Israelites come up with the idea of making the calf, but they have completely different reactions to its creation in the two texts. Exodus amplifies the people's sin; they express no remorse for what they have done, and their only two lines of dialogue in the chapter demonstrate the depth of their depravity. They approach Aaron about making the calf by stating, "Come, make gods for us, who shall go before us; as for this Moses, the man who brought us up out of the land of Egypt, we do not know what has become of him" (Exod 32:1). These words express their acceptance of other gods and their rejection of the one God, who has led them since their dramatic departure from Egypt through the sea. Their only other words exacerbate their problem by indeed claiming that it was the calf that rescued them from enslavement. When they exclaim, "These are your gods, O Israel, who brought you up out of the land of Egypt!" (Exod 32:4), they completely disavow the covenant that was established between themselves and God just a few chapters earlier. The Israelites of the Book of Exodus never express remorse or sorrow for the creation of the calf, but, as he does in the Qur'an, Moses seeks forgiveness and mercy from God in the aftermath of the golden calf event and God grants both.

In the qur'anic version of the story, the message about God's forgiveness and mercy is more streamlined in that as soon as the people sin, they repent, seek forgiveness, and receive it. There, the people speak less than they do in the Bible, but their one line puts them in a very different light than does their speech in Exodus: "If our Lord will not have mercy on us and forgive us our sins, we will surely be among the lost ones" (v. 149). Speaking the same words as Adam and Eve (Q 7:23) and Noah (Q 11:47), they recognize their offense, immediately ask God's forgiveness for their mistake, and do so on their own before Moses has returned to them from the mountain. The only other reference to them in the text is when Aaron tells Moses that the people threatened him and forced him to do what he did not want to do (v. 150). The Qur'an does not report exactly what happened to the people after this, but the comment in verse 153 that God shows mercy toward those who repent after sinning suggests that they were forgiven for their mistake after expressing remorse. In this way, the Israelites of the Qur'an experience an immediate return to God's favor, in contrast to their counterparts in Exodus who were eventually assured of God's forgiveness and ongoing mercy but would continue to test it in their wilderness journey.

Aaron

Moses's brother is not mentioned by name in the Qur'an, but elsewhere in the text he is identified as Aaron, so there is no doubt as to his identity. Just prior to this passage Moses instructs Aaron to take care of the people while he is away, but he is unable to live up to that task (Q 7:142). When Moses returns and sees the calf, he grabs Aaron by the hair, but his brother distances himself from what the people have done by claiming he was too weak to overcome them. He also refers to Moses as "son of my mother" to stress their fraternal relationship and to appeal to their familial bond (v. 150). This strategy appears to work because Moses immediately offers a prayer to God on behalf of both of them that includes the words "my brother" (v. 151). Nothing that Aaron states in the Qur'an is directly contradicted by the events of the story. The text says that the people built the calf, and it does not assign Aaron any role in its creation (v. 148). If he is guilty of a sin in the Qur'an it is one of omission, not commission, because he did not stop the people from making the calf.

This is not the role Aaron plays in the biblical version, where his guilt permeates the entire passage. At the outset of the narrative Aaron agreeably complies with the Israelites' request that he make them a calf, and there is no sense that he is being pressured or forced against his will (Exod 32:1–3). He then builds a mold, shapes the idol, and calls for a feast (Exod 32:4–5). When Moses confronts Aaron about what happened, he attempts to shift the blame to the people and offers what is arguably the most laughable excuse recorded in the Bible: "So I said to them, 'Whoever has gold, take it off'; so they gave it to me, and I threw it into the fire, and out came this calf!" (Exod 32:24). This claim of innocence fails to convince because Aaron was personally involved every step of the way in the design and construction of the calf, so his sin in the Bible is one of commission.

The Qur'an avoids directly implicating Aaron in the making of the calf for an important reason—he is considered to be a prophet in Islam and that is not the way a prophet would behave. Presented in a way that coheres to the standard of conduct expected of someone who has been chosen by God to play that special role, the Islamic Aaron is mentioned in the golden calf story but is kept a step removed from the actual construction of the idol.

Moses

Moses's actions unfold differently in the two versions of the story, supporting the thematic emphasis of each. While still on the mountain in the biblical account, Moses reminds God about the covenant with the Israelites and convinces the deity not to destroy the people for their sin (Exod 32:7–14). But once he descends and sees for himself what the people have done, Moses becomes enraged, and his fury over their sin intensifies as the story develops. In this way, his character here resonates with the biblical prophets—and the books that echo their perspectives—who interpreted the multiple massive destructions that the Israelites endured at the hands of the Assyrian and Babylonian armies: these were seen as punishment for Israel's breaking of the covenant. When Moses sees the calf and its accompanying revelry, he smashes the tablets that contain the law he has just received from God, symbolizing the rupture of the covenantal relationship (Exod 32:19). He then burns and pulverizes the calf and forces the people to drink the water into which he mixes the powder (Exod 32:20). After his conversation with Aaron he enlists the members of the tribe of Levi to attack those responsible for the calf, and the ensuing carnage results in the deaths of three thousand Israelites (Exod 32:25–29).[5] Only after this triple display of his indignation does Moses begin a series of interchanges with God, which eventually bring God's forgiveness and promise of enduring mercy. The dramatic crescendo of violent punishment in the story followed by a gradual process of reconciliation would have served as a point of identification for the generations of Israelites who listened to this story after enduring actual devastation, hoping for a restoration that seemed long in coming. In this way, the story arguably would have helped them to imagine that God's forgiveness and promise of enduring mercy might also be available to them.

In the Qur'an's version, Moses shifts rapidly from anger to compassion. He is furious when he returns to the people, and his ire is expressed through the double action of throwing down the tablets and grabbing Aaron by his hair (v. 150). But once he hears his brother's explanation and sees the people's repentance, his mood dramatically changes. Rather than lash out further at the people, he utters a prayer: "My Lord, forgive me and my brother and bring us into Your mercy, You who are the most merciful of all" (v. 151). Moses prays for himself and for Aaron, but not for the people because they have already expressed remorse and have asked forgiveness. Moses admits that he and his brother are to blame because they have not guided their people the way prophets should, and so they are in need of God's mercy. That need is highlighted at the end of the verse in the original Arabic, where three of the last five words come from a root that means "to have mercy" (*rahima*).[6] The passage concludes by stating that Moses's anger has subsided, and it describes him picking up the tablets that he had cast aside in his rage. Unlike the tablets in Exodus, they remain undamaged, and the text calls attention to the fact that they contain the very mercy (*rahmah*) he has sought for himself and his brother (v. 154).[7]

God

The divine character is also a study in contrasts in the two versions of the story. Every character asks for and promptly receives God's mercy in the Qur'an as each relationship is repaired and restored. This pattern supports the underlying Islamic emphasis on the availability of divine mercy to those who seek it. Soon after they construct the calf the people see the error of their ways and offer a prayer in which they acknowledge that their only hope lies in God's forgiveness: "If our Lord will not have mercy on us and forgive us our sins, we will surely be among the lost ones" (v. 149). As noted earlier, the comment (v. 153) that God is merciful toward wrongdoers who repent speaks directly to the people's situation and guarantees them a favorable response to their prayer. The same can be said about the other prayer uttered in the passage, the one from Moses on behalf of himself and Aaron (v. 151). It makes multiple appeals to divine mercy and forgiveness, indicating that the two prophet-brothers were also pardoned for their mistakes. Over the course of the relatively brief Qur'an passage, the various rifts among the characters are healed, and the cause of this transformation can be identified in two Arabic roots that are used repeatedly—words related to the root that means "to have mercy" (*rahima*) appear six times, and terms from the one that means "to forgive" (*ghafara*) are found three times.

The Exodus version portrays God, much as it portrays Moses, in a way that expands the dimension of sin and violent punishment before shifting gradually to forgiveness and mercy. After Moses's initial plea that God forgive the people (Exod 32:31–32), God responds with only punishment (Exod 32:33–35), and it takes three forms: only those who have sinned will be destroyed; God will not accompany the people in the desert but send an angel instead; and God "strikes" the people (which may indicate some form of illness). Before this point, three thousand Israelites had already lost their lives at the hands of the Levites, an attack that Moses said was a direct order from the deity (Exod 32:27). In the dialogue with Moses that ensues, God eventually reverses the decision not to accompany the people (Exod 33:14, 17), and demonstrates reconciliation with the people by writing a new set of tablets and affirming enduring mercy and love to the Israelites (Exod 34:1–9).

Overall observations

The versions of the story in both the Qur'an and Exodus convey the importance of remaining in right relationship with God, seeking forgiveness from God after sin, and trusting in God's enduring commitment to be merciful. The differences between the texts reflect interpretations suited to the ancient audience of each.

In its ancient context, the Exodus story addressed Israelites who struggled to keep their covenant with God, especially after multiple military devastations that were interpreted as justified punishments from God. By describing their ancestors as enduring similar struggles, the Exodus story would have resonated with Israelite hearers who were experiencing such struggles. Before it invites the audience to imagine God as committed to remain with the Israelites and to be gracious and merciful to them, the story emphasizes the people's propensity to disobey God's will and so to suffer the consequences. The message being conveyed might be captured in this way: "Yes, your struggles are severe, but God has proven capable of renewing the covenant after such struggles with sin and punishment in the past, so trust that God can do so now!"

The Islamic text addresses its message to all humanity and interprets the biblical tradition by highlighting the fundamental possibility of divine mercy and forgiveness for sin if people subsequently repent and seek mercy. The Israelites, Aaron, and Moses all fall short in the Qur'an, but without hesitation they all attempt to correct their errors by admitting their shortcomings. It is not as if the early Muslims did not struggle with sin or adversity, but unlike the Hebrew Bible traditions discussed above, the Qur'an does not interpret the believers' earthly suffering as punishment for their sins. In keeping with this pattern, its golden calf story seeks to focus hearers' imaginations on the constant invitation to submit to God in all things and to trust in God's mercy.

Further Biblical Interpretations

Moses is mentioned in the Hebrew Bible approximately one hundred times outside the Pentateuch, but most of these passages do not engage in interpretation of the traditions associated with him. An exception is a passage in Psalm 106, which is primarily concerned with the history of how the Israelites rebelled against God and violated the covenant. One section of the psalm refers to the golden calf episode as a time when they forgot God and Moses had to come to their rescue to prevent them from being destroyed (Ps 106:19–23). The passage presents the near devastation of the people as a justified punishment for their sins, and it is therefore in agreement with the final form of the golden calf story in Exodus. The psalm further interprets the Exodus story by envisioning Moses as a savior figure who turns back God's wrath from harming the Israelites. This ignores the role Moses plays in convincing the Levites to take up the sword and kill three thousand fellow Israelites (Exod 32:25–29), thus emphasizing Moses as a model prophet capable of effectively interceding for the people when they suffer because of their sin.

Of the several New Testament texts that allude to key episodes in Moses's life, the first book of the New Testament, the Gospel of Matthew, does so the most. It associates Jesus with Moses throughout. This Gospel opens with an account of Jesus's birth, weaving into it an interpretation of Moses. Mary and Joseph flee to Egypt with the newborn Jesus to avoid King Herod's decree that all children in Bethlehem under two years of age should be put to death (Matt 2:13–18). Although Moses is not referred to by name, the powerful ruler's edict to kill the infants and the reference to Egypt establish a close connection between the birth stories of Moses and Jesus. Early chapters of Matthew recount how Jesus passed through the waters of baptism, spent forty days in the wilderness where he was tempted by the devil, and then delivered the Sermon on the Mount in which he taught about the law (Matt 3—7). These events recall how Moses led the people through the waters of the exodus, spent forty years wandering with them in the wilderness, and ascended Mount Sinai, where he received the law and presented it to the people. This Gospel presents Jesus as a Moses figure in order to communicate to its Jewish audience that Jesus was the Messiah whom they anticipated would be sent by God.[8]

Moses appears by name in one New Testament scene that is described in each of the three Synoptic Gospels (Matt 17:1–8; Mark 9:2–8; Luke 9:28–36). Jesus takes three of his disciples to a mountain where his appearance is transformed in a dazzling way in front of them. During this episode, known as the transfiguration, Moses and Elijah miraculously appear with Jesus and begin speaking with him. They represent the central Jewish scriptural collections of the Law and the Prophets, respectively. Of the three, only Jesus is transformed in appearance, and the presence of these two venerable authorities of the past legitimates the uniquely important identity of Jesus in continuity with Jewish tradition.

In a scene recounted only in the Gospel of John (3:1–21), Jesus compares himself to Moses while conversing with a Jewish leader named Nicodemus. In the course of their conversation, Jesus says, "And just as Moses lifted up the serpent in the wilderness, so must the Son of Man be lifted up, that whoever believes in him may have eternal life" (John 3:14–15). This refers to an event involving Moses described in Numbers 21. During their journey as described in Exodus and Numbers from Egypt to Mount Sinai, and from there to Canaan, the Israelites complain about the conditions of the journey multiple times. God initially responds by feeding them, but after they have agreed to the covenant with God at Mount Sinai, their complaints are interpreted as lack of trust and they are punished. In the final episode of such complaint (Num 21:4–9), God sends snakes to kill the people. However, the people confess their sin and Moses petitions God for their healing. Following God's instructions, Moses fashions a bronze serpent and puts it on a pole, and whoever looks upon the serpent is healed. With the words of Jesus quoted above, the writer of John interprets this episode as a parallel to Jesus's death on a cross, which lifts him up like the serpent and leads to the salvation of those who look upon (i.e., believe in) him. In this way, John employs the

Moses tradition to convey an understanding of Christ as one who can save all.

Before turning to Paul's interpretation of Moses, it is important to stress that his use of negative rhetoric in 1–2 Corinthians to portray God's covenant with the Jewish people is best kept in the context of his main purpose, which is to portray the value of the new covenant in Christ. Many contemporary Christians affirm the ongoing validity of God's covenant with the Jewish people.[9]

In 2 Corinthians 3, Paul cites a tradition involving Moses. In Exodus 34:29–35, Moses's face begins to shine when he is speaking with God on Mount Sinai, and—perhaps because they were afraid of the glow—he wears a veil when in the presence of the Israelites. Paul interprets this scene in an argument that he constructs to underscore the value of the new covenant established by Christ. Paul presents the covenant of Moses in negative terms, doing so as a rhetorical strategy to demonstrate the value of the new covenant in Christ.

> [10]Indeed, what once had glory has lost its glory because of the greater glory; [11]for if what was set aside came through glory, much more has the permanent come in glory! [12]Since, then, we have such a hope, we act with great boldness, [13]not like Moses, who put a veil over his face to keep the people of Israel from gazing at the end of the glory that was being set aside. [14]But their minds were hardened. Indeed, to this very day, when they hear the reading of the old covenant, that same veil is still there, since only in Christ is it set aside. [15]Indeed, to this very day whenever Moses is read, a veil lies over their minds; [16]but when one turns to the Lord, the veil is removed. (2 Cor 3:10–16)

While in Exodus the image of Moses needing a veil indicated the special relationship he had with God, Paul here gives it a negative connotation by saying that the glory on Moses's face was ending, being set aside. Paul then transfers the motif of the veil from the one that covered Moses's face to a metaphoric veil that he contends prevents Jews from recognizing the value of the new covenant.

Paul interprets Moses also in his First Letter to the Corinthians, in a section that uses the Israelites both to anticipate future Christian practice and to warn Paul's audience against idolatry.

> [1]I do not want you to be unaware, brothers and sisters, that our ancestors were all under the cloud, and all passed through the sea, [2]and all were baptized into Moses in the cloud and in the sea, [3]and all ate the same spiritual food, [4]and all drank the same spiritual drink. For they drank from the spiritual rock that followed them, and the rock was Christ. [5]Nevertheless, God was not pleased with most of them, and they were struck down in the wilderness. (1 Cor 10:1–5)

In this passage Paul draws upon a number of events in Moses's life. The cloud refers to the pillar of cloud from God that went before the Israelites during daylight hours after they left Egypt (Exod 13:21). The passing through the sea is an obvious allusion to the exodus (Exod 14—15). The spiritual food and drink are the manna and water God provided the Israelites during their wanderings, and the spiritual rock describes the source from which that water flowed (Exod 16:4–35; 17:1–7; Num 20:7–11). Paul adds some unexpected twists that reveal his purpose in mentioning these traditions. Paul reads these stories as anticipations of the baptism and ongoing faith that was experienced by his Christian audience, and as a warning against overconfidence. He says that their ancestors were baptized into Moses through the cloud and the sea, something that is not mentioned in the Hebrew Bible. Similarly, he identifies the rock that produced water with Christ. As Christians understood themselves to be baptized into Christ, Paul presents the Israelites as baptized into Moses when they passed through the sea. As Christians participate in the body and blood of Christ (2 Cor 10:16–17), the ancient Israelites drank the life-giving water of Christ, even if they did not know it.

Focus for Comparison

Thematically, both the Bible and Qur'an interpret the traditions of Moses and the golden calf in ways that emphasize the importance of turning from sin to receive God's forgiveness and mercy, but the biblical traditions do so with a more expansive treatment of sin and punishment. As seen in its versions of both Moses's birth story and the golden calf episode, the Islamic text's interpretation primarily highlights God's role in the events and focuses attention on divine mercy.

Both the Qur'an and the New Testament draw parallels between each religion's originating figure and Moses, but the latter does this in a way that is more expansive, directly linking Moses and Jesus in various ways: presenting Jesus as a second Moses (Matthew's birth story and Sermon on the Mount), including a scene in which both appear so Moses can legitimate Jesus (the transfiguration), and citing events from Moses's life that anticipate the coming of Jesus (1 Corinthians). This difference makes sense in light of how Islam and Christianity differ in understanding the Torah of Moses; while Muslims understand it is a revelation from God that was misunderstood by Jews, among the Christians who wrote the New Testament were many Jews who believed that the life, death, and resurrection of Jesus fulfilled Moses's teaching.

Questions to Consider

1. Which is more obvious to you: the similarities or the differences in how Moses is presented in the Bible and the Qur'an?

2. Why might it be that God is not mentioned in the Exodus account of Moses's birth?

3. Which character do you think is most dramatically changed by the Qur'an's telling of the golden calf story?

4. Does it seem strange that Aaron is considered to be a prophet in Islam?

5. How might the expansive treatment of sin and punishment in the golden calf story as told in Exodus and in Psalm 106 have met a need in the ancient Israelite audience?

6. What do you think might have been the purpose of leaving extensive treatment of punishment out of the Qur'an version of the golden calf story?

7. What is your response to how the New Testament interprets the Moses traditions?

CHAPTER 7

David and Saul

The Qur'an devotes much less attention to David than does the Bible. The Bible recounts his life over the course of forty-two chapters in three books (1 Samuel, 2 Samuel, and 1 Kings), and more briefly in 1 Chronicles 11—29. By contrast, the Qur'an mentions David by name only sixteen times, and some of those references occur in lists of prophetic figures that do not describe him in any detail. In addition, the aspects of David's life that are treated in the two texts differ considerably. The Hebrew Bible devotes much attention to David's rise to the kingship from humble origins, his complicated relationship with his predecessor Saul and his family, and David's time on the throne, but the Qur'an has little to say about these matters. Nevertheless, there is some overlap in how the biblical narrative and the Qur'an present King David, and of the episodes from David's life treated in both, the present chapter discusses two—the battle with Goliath and Nathan's parable.

In addition to specific episodes from David's life, both the Qur'an and the Bible associate David with psalms and expressions of praise. Within the biblical canon, nearly half of the 150 psalms are associated with David through superscriptions, brief texts that appear above the psalm but are not part of its lyric text. More than a dozen of such superscriptions connect a psalm to specific moments or circumstances in his life. Islam associates the Book of Psalms with David, as the Qur'an maintains that the book was given to him by God, making him one of just a handful of prophets who have received a revealed text from the deity (Q 4:163; 17:55).[1] Passages in which elements of the natural world were compelled to offer glory to God along with David echo language in the psalms where the natural world extols God's majesty: "We made the mountains and the birds praise us with David" (Q 21:79b; cf. 34:10).

In addition, the Qur'an describes David in several specific ways. It recounts that God gave David his son Solomon, knowledge (Q 27:15), and the ability to distinguish truth from falsehood (Q 38:20). God also softened iron for David, which allowed him to make coats of mail and weapons for battle (Q 21:80; 34:10–11). It is perhaps because of his role as a prophet who has received a book and has been blessed by God that David is referred to in the Qur'an as a caliph (*khalīfah*), or vice regent, a title that is otherwise bestowed only on Adam (Q 38:26; cf. 2:30).

The Battle with Goliath

David's defeat of the Philistine giant Goliath is the celebrated feat that launches his career in the Bible (1 Sam 17), and the Qur'an contains a clear, if somewhat abbreviated, reference to it. It is preceded by the Islamic text's only mention of Saul, in a passage that sets the stage for David's arrival on the scene.

[246]Have you not considered the leaders of the Children of Israel who came after Moses? They said to a prophet among them, "Raise up a king for us that we might fight in God's way." He said, "Is it possible that you would not fight if you were told to do so?" They replied, "How can we not fight in the way of God when we have been expelled from our homes and separated from our children?" But when they were ordered to fight, all but a few of them turned back. God knows who the evildoers are. [247]Their prophet said to them, "God has raised up Saul as king for you." They responded, "How can he be king over us when we have more right to authority than he does, and great wealth has not been given to him?" He said, "God has chosen him over you and has greatly increased his knowledge and stature. God gives His kingdom to whomever He pleases for God is

all-embracing and all-knowing." [248]Their prophet continued, "The sign of his kingship is that the ark will come to you. In it will be assurance from your Lord and relics left behind by the family of Moses and the family of Aaron, carried by angels. Truly, there is a sign in that for those of you who believe." [249]As Saul went out with his army he said, "God will test you at a river. Those who drink from it will not be with me, but those who do not drink from it will be with me, except for the one who scoops it up with his hand." But they all drank from it except for a few of them. When he and those who believed with him crossed the river they said, "We have no strength today against Goliath and his army." But those who thought they would meet God said, "A small group has often overcome a larger one with God's permission. God is with those who remain steadfast!" [250]When they went out to Goliath and his army they said, "Our Lord, make us steadfast, steady our feet, and help us against the unbelievers!" [251]Then they defeated them with God's permission, and David killed Goliath. God gave him power and wisdom, and He taught him what He pleased. If God did not defeat some people by means of others the world would truly be corrupt, but God is generous to all. (Q 2:246–51)

COMPARISON WITH THE BIBLICAL NARRATIVE

Saul's name in the Qur'an is Talut (*ṭālūt*; "the tall one"), and this section has connections to a number of biblical scenes that feature him. The story is set after the time of Moses, and it begins with the Israelites asking an unnamed prophet to appoint a king over them. In extraqur'anic Islamic sources, that prophet is identified as Samuel, who plays a role similar to the one he has in the Bible when he reluctantly acquiesces to the Israelites' demand that they be given a king (1 Sam 8). Like the Qur'an, the biblical tradition also refers to Saul's height, his humble origins, and the Israelites' unwillingness to accept Saul as their leader (v. 247; 1 Sam 9:2, 21; 10:27).

In both texts David defeats and kills Goliath, and despite the brevity of the Qur'an's account of the battle, it contains a couple of elements that are also found in the biblical version. One is the initial reaction of fear on the part of the Israelites as they calculate their odds against such a superior foe. The biblical story twice calls attention to the terror they feel before the enemy. As Goliath taunts them and demands that one of them should engage him one-on-one, their hearts sink (1 Sam 17:11). A bit later Goliath emerges a second time and repeats the same message, and they have a similar reaction. "All the Israelites, when they saw the man, fled from him and were very much afraid" (1 Sam 17:24). This mirrors the initial reaction of Saul's depleted army in the Qur'an when they acknowledge their underdog status (v. 249). These initial feelings of despair and hopelessness on the part of the Israelites are replaced in both 1 Samuel and the Qur'an with a sense of confidence that God is on their side. Once the biblical David arrives on the scene, he boldly proclaims three times that the Philistines do not stand a chance because the deity will lead him and his fellow Israelites to victory (1 Sam 17:45–47; cf. 1 Sam 17:26; 36–37). In the same way, the Israelites in the Qur'an exhibit a change in perspective as they turn to God and their initial desperation is transformed into a conviction that all is not lost (vv. 249–50).

The Qur'an's treatment of Saul in the test at the river that results in the size of his army being greatly diminished (v. 249) also parallels a biblical account found not in the biblical Saul traditions but in the biblical Book of Judges. In this account, set in a time prior to Saul, the size of Gideon's army is greatly reduced by means of a trial at a river (Judg 7:4–8), and as in the Qur'an (v. 249), God is the one behind the test. Despite the fact that they are greatly outnumbered, the Israelites and Gideon are able to defeat the enemy, and their victory can only be attributed to divine assistance.

INTERPRETATION OF DAVID AND SAUL

The Ark of the Covenant

The Qur'an's mention of the ark of the covenant in this passage reveals several distinctive elements. The biblical stories concerning the time of Saul and David imagine the ark as a simple, wooden, box-shaped object that symbolized God's presence among the Israelites and was carried into battle (cf. Deut 10:1–5). The texts of the Pentateuch associated with the Priestly sources describe in much more ornate terms the ark that was carried in procession during the desert wandering and housed in the portable sanctuary as a forerunner of the one that would be preserved in the Jerusalem temple built by Solomon (cf. Exod 25:10–22). Sometimes calling it "the ark of God," "the ark of the Lord," or simply "the ark," the Bible most often refers to this container as the "ark of the covenant," reflecting the tradition that it contained the tablets of the law that Moses received from the deity upon entering the covenant with the Israelites (Exod 25:16; Deut 10:1–2). Compared to over two hundred references to the ark in the Bible, the present story contains the only mention of the ark in the Qur'an, referring to it simply as "the ark" (v. 248). The relative lack of interest in the ark and the absence of the term *covenant* from the reference reflect the little importance that the Qur'an accords to the covenant between God and Israel (discussed in Chapter 6 regarding Moses).

In the present story, Samuel informs the Israelites that Saul's legitimacy as king will be verified by his possession of the ark and what it contains. The Bible, however, does not make any connection between Saul's reign and the ark of the covenant, which was captured by the Philistines prior to his rise to power (1 Sam 4), and it was David who rescued it from them and returned it to the Israelites (2 Sam 6). The Qur'an's reference to angels carrying the ark could be an allusion to the cherubim that adorned it in the Priestly description (Exod 25:17–20), in effect conflating the two biblical descriptions of the ark. Although this is the only mention of the ark in the Qur'an, the same Arabic word (*tābūt*) is used elsewhere to describe the basket that Moses's mother placed him in to protect him from Pharaoh (Q 20:39).[2]

An important quality of the ark in the historical books of the Bible is that it embodies the divine presence in a practical way. When the Israelites brought it out on the battlefield with them, it served as a concrete manifestation of God's presence fighting alongside them. One function of imagining the ark in this way would have been to give confidence to the Israelite army. The deity's presence with them during war did not guarantee victory for them, however, since the presumption was that their obedience to

God was the determinative factor. This explains why God allowed the Philistines to defeat the Israelites and take possession of the ark from them in 1 Samuel 4. Islamic views on the nature of God preclude such a concrete understanding of the divine presence, but they share the notion that the ark symbolized an assurance of God's help and possibly of God's presence.

The contents of the ark that are listed in this passage include something translated here as "assurance" (*sakīna*). The Arabic term appears six times in the Qur'an, and in each case involves a passage related to warfare or fighting where its purpose is to strengthen or give confidence to those in battle (cf. Q 9:26, 40; 48:4, 18, 26). This is the only passage in which the term is found in something like the ark, and in every passage it is sent down by God or referred to as "His." The word comes from an Arabic root whose primary sense is "to dwell, to inhabit," and the meaning "assurance" reflects the way in which a house or dwelling is a place of comfort and peace.

A translation of the term that conveys more directly the sense of dwelling might be more appropriate for these Qur'an verses because they might intend to describe God's presence with those on the battlefield. This alternative is appealing because there are words that are etymologically close to *sakīna* in Hebrew and Aramaic, two languages related to Arabic, that describe the divine presence. For example, the postbiblical Hebrew term *shekinah* refers to God's manifestation in the world. If these Qur'an passages intend such a sense, then they are calling attention to the deity's role as a strengthening and supporting presence for those who engage in battle. The word might therefore be describing God rather than tranquility or some other quality that the deity imparts on people. The former alternative is usually not accepted by translators of the Qur'an because it is in tension with beliefs about divine transcendence and unity that are central to Islamic theology.

According to verse 148 the ark also contained relics belonging to the Israelites, who are identified as the families of Moses and Aaron. The objects are not specified, but some Islamic commentators have suggested they included Moses's sandals and Aaron's staff. One biblical tradition reports that Aaron's staff was deposited in the tent of the covenant, the place where the ark was housed (Num 17:8–11), while the New Testament Letter to the Hebrews claims that the staff was kept in the ark (Heb 9:4). Whatever the precise nature of the contents of the ark, the Qur'an leaves no doubt about its symbolic role because the verse mentions twice that it was meant to serve as a sign for all believers.

Saul, David, and Goliath

David's defeat of Goliath, one of the most detailed biblical battle scenes, pays great attention to what each is wearing (or not) and the weapons they employ (1 Sam 17:5–7, 38–40). In addition, the text reports their harsh exchange of words as they trade insults, each attempting to belittle his opponent (1 Sam 17:8–10, 42–47). The gory description of Goliath's death explains how he is knocked senseless by David's slingshot and then beheaded with his own sword (1 Sam 17:48–51). In keeping with its usual sparse style, the Qur'an mentions none of these details, condensing the drama and tension of the biblical account to three words in both Arabic and English—"David killed Goliath" (v. 251).[3]

The Islamization of the biblical traditions about Saul and David appears in multiple ways in this passage. As it does in other biblically related texts, the Qur'an presents the story about the battle with Goliath in a way that recalls the circumstances of the Prophet Muhammad's life and the context of the early Muslim community. According to the Islamic sources, many of his contemporaries in Mecca were reluctant to accept Muhammad as a legitimate prophet, and this is similar to what Saul experienced when the people of Israel responded to Samuel (v. 247). One of the charges leveled against Muhammad by some of the Meccans was that he was insane and the messages he claimed to be receiving from God were a figment of his imagination. One passage reassures him that this was not the case (Q 68:2–6; cf. 15:6). In another passage, his enemies call attention to Muhammad's relative poverty and lack of social status in a way similar to what Saul's detractors said about him (Q 34:34–36). By highlighting the negative reception Saul received, the Qur'an offers words of encouragement and comfort to Muhammad and attempts to frame his rejection as a sign of his legitimate authority.

In a similar way, the situation the Israelites faced when they lined up against enemy forces that considerably outnumbered them mirrors closely the circumstances the Muslim community confronted in some of its early battles. When Saul's followers note how small they are in comparison to Goliath's forces (v. 249), they could be describing what took place at the Battle of Badr in 624 CE, which is mentioned in the Qur'an: "God helped you at Badr when you were weak and vulnerable. Be mindful of God, that you may give thanks" (Q 3:123). The Badr encounter took place at a small town on the Red Sea about one hundred miles southwest of Medina. A Meccan caravan was returning home when a group of three hundred Muslims attacked it and plundered its goods. In response, more than one thousand Meccan troops were dispatched to defend the caravan, but despite their numerical advantage they were routed by the Muslims. This Qur'an verse interprets the Badr victory as a sign that God was on the side of the faithful, if numerically disadvantaged, Muslim army. The story of Israelites preparing for their battle against Goliath and his group makes the same point.

A similar connection to the early Islamic community appears in the question that the Israelites direct to Samuel: "How can we not fight in the way of God when we have been expelled from our homes and separated from our children?" (v. 246). This statement does not fit the context of the biblical story of Saul because the Israelites have been in the land of Canaan for generations and have not been expelled from it. However, it does reflect the situation of the group of Muhammad's early followers, who were not welcome in their hometown of Mecca and were forced to flee for their lives in 622 CE to the northern town of Yathrib (later known as Medina), where they were able to thrive and flourish. Presenting the Israelites as enduring a similar situation and overcoming obstacles that appear insurmountable would have been a source of strength and comfort for the early Muslims.

The last sentence of the passage offers a final example of the Islamization of the Saul and David traditions. Immediately after David kills Goliath it states, "If God did not defeat some people by means of others the world would truly be corrupt, but God is generous to all" (v. 251). As in other places in the Qur'an, this statement universalizes the meaning of the text and interprets its relevance for all people. By comparison with the Bible, the Islamic text is much more explicit about making plain the lesson or teaching it seeks to convey. It provides a summary statement that encapsulates its main point and highlights the implications for all who read it. In this way, the qur'anic story of David and Goliath is as much about the present as it is about the past. As seen in the exilic/postexilic editing of the golden calf story discussed in the chapter on Moses, many biblical stories also address the situation of the ancient audience. However, indications in the text that this is happening are typically more subtle in the biblical literature than in the Qur'an.

David's Encounter with the Litigants

In another passage that echoes an episode in David's life, one recounted in 2 Samuel 12, the Qur'an describes a conversation between David and two men who visit him that results in his admitting wrongdoing and seeking God's mercy.[4]

> [21]Have you heard the story of the litigants who climbed the wall into the private quarters? [22]When they came upon David he was startled, but they said, "Do not fear. We are two litigants, and one of us has treated the other unfairly. Judge between us in truth, and lead us to the right path. [23]This is my brother. He has ninety-nine ewes, and I have only one. He said, 'Let me take care of her,' and he intimidated me with his words." [24]David said, "He has clearly mistreated you by demanding your ewe in addition to his own. Many partners treat each other unfairly except for those who are faithful and act righteously, but they are very few." Then David realized We were testing him, and he asked forgiveness from his Lord, fell on his knees, and repented. [25]So we forgave him for that, and he is indeed close to Us and has a good final abode. [26]"Oh David, We have made you ruler over the land. Judge truthfully between people and do not follow your own desires, or it will lead you away from God's path. A harsh punishment awaits those who stray

from God's path because they have forgotten the Day of Reckoning." (Q 38:21–26)

The relevant biblical passage occurs immediately after the account of David's affair with Bathsheba in 2 Samuel 11. When he learns she is expecting his child, David summons Bathsheba's husband Uriah from the battlefield, assuming that he will have sexual relations with his wife and all will assume that Uriah is the father of the child. Out of loyalty to his fellow soldiers, Uriah refuses to go home and enjoy the company of Bathsheba, and so David decides to arrange for Uriah's death. His plan works; Uriah is killed in battle after being placed in a vulnerable position, and once the required period of mourning comes to an end, David marries Bathsheba.

David believes he has avoided personal scandal, but soon after the birth of his son the prophet Nathan pays him a visit to inform him that God is displeased with what David has done. Yet, rather than accuse David directly, Nathan tells him a parable that causes David to point his finger back at himself.

> [1]There were two men in a certain city, the one rich and the other poor. [2]The rich man had very many flocks and herds; [3]but the poor man had nothing but one little ewe lamb, which he had bought. He brought it up, and it grew up with him and with his children; it used to eat of his meager fare, and drink from his cup, and lie in his bosom, and it was like a daughter to him. [4]Now there came a traveler to the rich man, and he was loath to take one of his own flock or herd to prepare for the wayfarer who had come to him, but he took the poor man's lamb, and prepared that for the guest who had come to him (2 Sam 12:1–4).

COMPARISON WITH THE BIBLICAL NARRATIVE

When David expresses outrage at what the rich man did and calls for his death, Nathan tells him that David is the guilty party, and that in anger over what he has done to Bathsheba and Uriah, God will bring upon David's own family and descendants trouble and tragedy, beginning with the death of his newborn son (2 Sam 12:5–15). David admits his sin and repents by fasting and prostrating himself before God, pleading that God might spare his son, but when the child dies David accepts what has happened and resumes normal activities (2 Sam 12:13–25). The biblical story of the two men is similar to the Qur'an passage despite obvious differences. Nathan plays no role in the Islamic story, or anywhere else in the Qur'an for that matter, as the two men of the parable personally pay a visit to David and speak directly to him. Similarly, neither Bathsheba nor Uriah is ever mentioned in the Qur'an, although this passage may allude to them. The Qur'an does not identify why David expresses remorse and asks God to forgive him (v. 24), but it likely assumes that its readers are familiar with the backstory involving Bathsheba and Uriah. This may also be the case with the deity's admonition that David should not follow his own desires because they will divert him from God's path (v. 26). The biblical story makes it clear that it was David's lust for Bathsheba that led him to commit adultery and have her husband murdered.

INTERPRETATION OF DAVID

In the Qur'an David delivers his verdict about who is at fault after hearing from only one of the two men. The text does not report what happens to the disputants after this because the focus shifts to David, who realizes he is being tested by God and immediately acknowledges his sin. The Islamic David does not need the assistance of someone like Nathan to recognize his mistake because he is a prophet who has a special relationship with God. It is unusual for the Qur'an to mention the shortcomings of a prophet, but the reference to David's repentance allows for the introduction of a central theme of the Qur'an—divine mercy. This passage reminds its readers that prophets are human beings who sometimes fall short and need God's forgiveness. The qur'anic text lacks the specificity of the biblical tradition regarding the nature of David's offense, but it still makes reference to it and leads to a different outcome. Whereas the David of the Bible and his offspring are punished by God for what David did despite his repentance, his Muslim counterpart repairs his relationship with the deity by admitting his mistake and seeking forgiveness. As a result, he is forgiven and brought closer to God (v. 25).[5]

Second Samuel shares many theological perspectives both with the Book of Deuteronomy and with the historical Books of Joshua, Judges, 1–2 Samuel, and 1–2 Kings. Hence, these six historical books are known collectively as the Deuteronomistic History, which like Deuteronomy (and the rest of the Pentateuch) was edited after the Babylonian exile in ways that interpret it as divine punishment for Israel's history of breaking covenant with God.[6] The account of David's sin regarding Bathsheba and Uriah echoes a perspective found throughout these books that is critical of the way Israelite kings abused power.

Further Biblical Interpretations

The description of David's rise to power and reign as king in the Books of 1–2 Samuel and 1 Kings is one of two accounts of his life preserved in the Bible, and we have already noted some of the interpretive elements present in it. This account served as a source for the other account, in 1 Chronicles 11—29, which was written later—most likely during the Persian period. The later version relates the events found in the earlier one in abbreviated form while also adding some elements. In contrast to the Deuteronomistic Historian's more critical perspective, the author(s) of 1–2 Chronicles, known as the Chronicler, presents a streamlined and cleaned-up version of things that puts David in a very positive light. For the Chronicler, writing at a time when the monarchy no longer existed but the temple remained central to the Jewish religious system, it was important to portray their heroic ancestor David as a model of piety who was directly involved in the Temple and its activities. For example, the story of David's affair with Bathsheba and his involvement in Uriah's death is completely missing in 1 Chronicles, although the part that describes David staying in Jerusalem rather than going out to battle is found in both texts (2 Sam 11:1; 1 Chr 20:1). The exclusion of the episode can be explained in that its presentation of David as a lustful murderer does not fit the image of him that the Chronicler constructs. In a similar interpretive move, one intended to endow David with a priestly character, 1 Chronicles 23—27 depicts David as personally involved in the design of the temple in Jerusalem and arranging many details related to the temple cult, even though the temple was not built until after he died. In the version of his reign in 2 Samuel and 1 Kings, David does none of this. There are many examples throughout 1 Chronicles of this tendency to burnish David's image and associate him with the temple and priestly activity.

As noted above, superscriptions on 73 of the 150 psalms in the Hebrew Bible relate those psalms to David. The most common superscription is simply "of David" and can be read as attributing authorship.[7] Thirteen of the superscriptions are more interpretive, referring to specific moments in David's life.[8] In these cases the content of the psalm is meant to suggest something about his feelings or state of mind at these key moments. For example, the opening lines of Psalm 51 convey a good sense of its genre as a poem of remorse and repentance.

> [1]Have mercy on me, O God,
>   according to your steadfast love;
>
> according to your abundant mercy
>   blot out my transgressions.
> [2]Wash me thoroughly from my iniquity,
>   and cleanse me from my sin.
>
> [3]For I know my transgressions,
>   and my sin is ever before me.
> [4]Against you, you alone, have I sinned,
>   and done what is evil in your sight,
> so that you are justified in your sentence
>   and blameless when you pass judgment.
> [5]Indeed, I was born guilty,
>   a sinner when my mother conceived me. (Ps 51:1–5)

The superscription of this psalm reads in part, "A psalm of David, when the prophet Nathan came to him, after he had gone in to

Bathsheba," but David is not mentioned in the psalm itself. The account of Nathan's visit to him after his affair with Bathsheba in 2 Samuel 12 does not contain these words from David. He acknowledges that he has sinned, fasts, and petitions unsuccessfully for the survival of his and Bathsheba's newborn son (2 Sam 12:13–19), but he does not explicitly express remorse or ask for forgiveness. The superscriptions were added long after the psalms were composed, and this one seeks to enhance David's status as a model of piety, attributing to him a level of regret and sorrow beyond what he exhibits in the narrative in 2 Samuel 12. Moreover, the psalm contains a clue that it was written much later than David's time in that it issues a call to "rebuild the walls of Jerusalem" (v. 18b)—something that would not have been necessary until the Babylonian destruction of the city nearly four centuries after his death.

The New Testament refers to David numerous times in support of an author's Christology, or view of Jesus. Several passages refer to him as "Son of David," a title Jesus in the Gospels never claims for himself and that likely identifies him as the Messiah.[9] Particularly prevalent in Matthew, this title introduces Jesus's genealogy in the very first verse of that Gospel. Perhaps the most well-known scene in which it is found is enacted liturgically by millions of Christians throughout the world annually on the Sunday before Easter, known as Passion Sunday or Palm Sunday. According to the Synoptic Gospels, as Jesus enters the city of Jerusalem just prior to his death he is greeted by crowds of people who proclaim,

> Hosanna to the Son of David!
> Blessed is the one who comes in the name of the Lord!
> Hosanna in the highest heaven! (Matt 21:9; cf.
>   Mark 11:9–10; Luke 19:36–38)

The figure of the Messiah has a complex history in ancient Judaism, but its association with David is certainly linked to the promise God made to him through the prophet Nathan that David's offspring would rule forever (2 Sam 7:12–16).

David's connection to Jesus's family tree in the Gospel of Matthew goes deeper than the mentions of his name in the genealogy (Matt 1:6). According to Matthew's presentation of it, Jesus's family line is divided into three sections that contain fourteen generations each (Matt 1:17).[10] The author arranged things this way in conformance with the ancient practice of gematria, a type of code whereby the letters in a word are assigned numbers that add up to a numerical total. If the first letter of the Hebrew alphabet represents the number one and each subsequent letter increases by one, the letters of David's name add up to fourteen. In this way, Matthew is able to convey the idea that Jesus truly is the Son of David who is the culmination of messianic expectations that have been passed down through generations.

Focus for Comparison

Both the Bible and the Qur'an interpret Davidic traditions by associating him with psalms, but the biblical Psalter takes its interpretation a step further by linking particular psalms with specific moments in David's life. Doing so makes David a model of piety by suggesting that these psalms provide a glimpse into David's interior life and state of mind as he had these various experiences. A more dramatic example of interpretation by the Bible appears when comparing its two versions of David's life. The account in 1 Chronicles, unlike that in the earlier Deuteronomistic History, contains nothing scandalous or negative that might blemish David's reputation as he is presented as a pious man above reproach, linked to temple and priestly ritual. In comparison, the Qur'an's portrayal of David remains consistent throughout—he was a prophet of God who faithfully delivered to his people the message he received. In this way, the Qur'an is similar to the New Testament: while the latter portrays Jesus as "son of David" to communicate his status as Messiah, the former portrays David as a faithful prophet and messenger, a forerunner of Muhammad.

Questions to Consider

1. What are the key similarities and differences in how the relationship between God and David is portrayed in the Bible and the Qur'an?

2. Why might the Goliath story be so much briefer in the Qur'an than in 1 Samuel?

3. Is it more likely that the ark in the Qur'an contains assurance or God's presence? Explain.

4. Is it unusual that Saul is compared to Muhammad even though he is not considered to be a prophet in Islam? Explain.

5. What is your reaction to the idea that the Qur'an's story of Saul is meant to respond to the experiences of early Muslims?

6. Do you think the story of the two litigants in the Qur'an is a parallel to the parable recounted in 2 Samuel 12?

7. What is your reaction to how David is interpreted in the New Testament?

CHAPTER 8

Solomon and the Queen of Sheba

Solomon is both a king and a prophet in the Qur'an, but he is never given the latter title in the Bible. There is more information in the Qur'an about Solomon than there is about his father David, which is the opposite of what is found in the Bible. Solomon is granted a number of special powers and abilities in the Islamic tradition that add a unique dimension to his character, and this is especially so regarding his relationships with animals and other nonhuman beings. This chapter will focus on how the Bible and the Qur'an recount the Queen of Sheba's visit to Solomon, but before turning to that we consider a couple of other passages that describe important aspects of his life.

Solomon's Horses

The following passage from the Qur'an focuses on the role of horses in Solomon's life and seems to interpret the biblical account in 1 Kings 10 and its relationship to the law of the king in Deuteronomy 17.[1]

> [30]We gave Solomon to David. He was an excellent servant and ever repentant. [31]When well-bred swift horses were brought to him in the evening, [32]he said, "I have

loved good things more than the remembrance of my Lord until the sun's setting. [33]Bring them back to me!" Then he began to stroke their legs and necks. [34]We tested Solomon and put a corpse on his throne. Then he repented [35]and said, "My Lord, forgive me and give me a kingdom that will not be fit for anyone but me. Truly, You are the one who provides." [36]So We subjected the wind to him, and it gently blew at his command wherever he wished. [37]And also the jinn, all the builders and divers among them, [38]and others bound in chains. [39]"This is Our gift, so give or withhold it as you wish." [40]He is indeed near to Us, and has a good place to return to. (Q 38:30–40)

The overall assessment of Solomon in this passage is quite positive: he is a faithful servant (v. 30) who seeks forgiveness (v. 35) and is blessed by God (v. 40). At the same time, in a couple of places it appears that Solomon is criticized for certain flaws he possessed. Some aspects of the passage are difficult to understand and interpret, and this ambiguity makes it difficult to know exactly what is being said about Solomon. Muslim commentators have proposed various ways of reading those parts of the text that are ambiguous.

The section of the passage that treats Solomon's interest in horses is a case in point (vv. 31–33). It is immediately followed by a reference to God's testing Solomon and the latter's prayer of repentance (vv. 34–35), so it is plausible to see the horses as somehow hindering his relationship with God. The Qur'an is likely interpreting a biblical legal tradition that prohibits any Israelite king from acquiring too many horses and wives or accumulating excessive wealth (Deut 17:16–17). This biblical "law of the king" itself is probably alluding to Solomon, whose many horses, opulent lifestyle, and hundreds of wives are mentioned at the end of the description of his reign (1 Kgs 10:23—11:3; cf. 1 Kgs 4:26–28). This passage leads directly into a condemnation of Solomon for loving foreign wives who turned his heart from God and prevented him from following God's statutes (1 Kgs 11:4–13). As noted in chapter 7 concerning David, 1 Kings is part of the Deuteronomistic History, which in many places criticizes Israelite kings for

131

their abuse of power. Among the themes shared by Deuteronomy and 1 Kings is an interpretation of the disaster of the Babylonian exile as collective punishment for how a long line of Israelite kings beginning with David and Solomon broke God's law. This biblical criticism of Solomon provides the backstory to why he repents and asks forgiveness in the Qur'an, something he does not do in the Bible.

Solomon's comment in verse 32 suggests his priorities have become skewed as he mistakes his devotion to his horses for worship of God. What Solomon does to the horses after he has them brought back to him is not completely clear. Many commentators see the verb "to stroke" as a euphemism for striking them down, and propose that he killed the horses because they distracted him from praying. Others put forward a less violent reading and say that he simply stroked the animals with affection. Another alternative proposes that Solomon branded the horses so that they would be marked for God. However the scene is understood, it is clear that his love of horses somehow became an impediment in Solomon's relationship with God.

How God responds to what Solomon does to his horses is not entirely clear (v. 34). He is tested somehow by having a jasad (*jasad*) placed on his throne, but that Arabic term can mean more than one thing. The word is commonly used to refer to a human body, but it can also describe a statue or image, such as the golden calf that was made by the Israelites during Moses's time (Q 7:148). Perhaps the jasad is meant to symbolize what would happen if Solomon were to disobey the law and not follow God's will. He would be removed from power and replaced as king. Understood this way, seeing the jasad causes him to have a change of heart and seek repentance, something he fails to do in the Bible. Although the jasad could be understood as a skeleton, it is better to interpret it as a corpse sitting on the throne that otherwise should be occupied by the king. Various ideas have been put forward about this corpse, including that it was an evil jinn, Solomon's son, or even Solomon himself after he had been weakened by disease so that he was near death. The text does not provide any information that might clarify the nature of the test; perhaps it was Solomon's obsession with his horses, but it is meant to serve as a reminder to him that he sits on the throne only with God's permission. The

Arabic verb here translated "repented" (*'anāba*) can also mean "return," and it can have either a theological or physical sense in this passage. It may be describing Solomon's repentance as he turns and prays to God, or it could be referring to his actual return after being away or his return to good health after having been sick.

The passage goes on to state that God gave Solomon power and authority over the wind and the jinn (vv. 36–37). This might be construed as a reaffirmation of God's favor for Solomon, who has now repented. The Arabic word used for the jinn is actually the plural of "Satan" (*shayāṭīn*). The term is found approximately twenty times in the Qur'an, and it sometimes refers to people or jinn who act like Satan by rejecting God and the prophets (Q 6:112; 21:82). Here, they are said to come under Solomon's control and are referred to as builders and divers. Their ability to build might be connected to the many building projects that are associated with Solomon in the Bible, including the temple and his palace (1 Kgs 5—7). This passage indicates that the king co-opted the jinn to assist in the completion of those projects. The description of some of the jinn as divers likely refers to how they helped him to extract seafood, pearls, and other valuable objects from beneath the ocean. The idea that some of the jinn were chained (v. 38) could be connected to the biblical theme that Solomon oppressed his own people through slave labor in order to realize his construction projects (1 Kgs 5:13–14; 9:15, 21; 12:1–4). This might be a shift on the part of the Qur'an that takes a biblical tradition critical of Solomon for enslaving his own people and softens it by making it a more acceptable action. Solomon's mastery of the wind is mentioned elsewhere in the Qur'an (Q 21:81; 34:12; 38:36), and it rounds out the idea that the deity gave the king authority over the land, the sea, and the air.

Not much in this passage has a direct association with the biblical account of Solomon's reign, but in both texts the king makes a request of God. In the Qur'an, he asks for a kingdom (v. 35), and this is what leads to his having authority over the jinn and elements of nature. The Bible, on the other hand, reports an episode in which God appears to Solomon in a dream and asks him what he would like. When he expresses his desire for wisdom and an understanding mind, the deity is pleased and grants these to him, in addition to wealth and fame (1 Kgs 3:3–15). The

Qur'an does not make any mention of the wisdom of Solomon, which is an important biblical theme. According to the Bible, it was Solomon's many foreign wives and concubines (as well as his attraction to horses) that led to his alienation from God and his ultimate undoing (1 Kgs 11), but the Qur'an does not specify any of his shortcomings beyond perhaps his attachment to his horses. This is in keeping with the Islamic tradition's tendency to present the prophets in a favorable and positive light. The Qur'an explicitly states that he was not a disbeliever (Q 2:102), and the passage above says that he often turned to God and he repented for any offenses he may have committed (vv. 30, 34).

Solomon and the Jinn, Winds, Birds, and Ants

A second summary statement of certain aspects of Solomon's reign, found in chapter 34 of the Qur'an, also refers to his mastery over the jinn and the wind.

> [12]And to Solomon [We subjugated] the wind. It took a month for it to go out, and a month for it to return. We also made a mountain of brass to flow for him, and there were jinn who worked for him with his Lord's permission. If one of them did not follow Our command, We would make him taste the punishment of the fire. [13]They made for him whatever he wished, including places of worship, statues, basins like cisterns, and fixed caldrons. "Give thanks in work, O house of David, for only a few of my servants are thankful." [14]When We decreed that Solomon should die, nothing indicated to them that he had died except for a small creature that ate away at his staff. When he fell over, the jinn realized that if they had known what was hidden from them they would not have continued with their humiliating work. (Q 34:12–14)

This passage calls attention to Solomon's building projects, but here it is the jinn who are forced into labor rather than humans as in the biblical version of events. The text is quick to point out that it is ultimately God and not the king who has authority over the jinn (v. 12), and this is in keeping with the qur'anic view that even the prophets must submit to the divine will. The report of Solomon's death is an unusual feature of this passage, and it too highlights his submission to the deity with the statement that God decreed his death. The description of the deceased ruler leaning on his staff until a small animal gnaws at it and causes his corpse to tumble to the ground is a criticism of the jinn that calls attention to their inferior intelligence and lack of knowledge (v. 14).

In addition to his power over the winds, the Qur'an notes that Solomon had a unique capacity to communicate with nonhuman creatures. This can be seen in a passage in which he mentions his ability to speak with birds and demonstrates a capacity to understand the language of ants.

> [16]Solomon inherited from David and said, "O people, we have been taught the speech of birds, and we have been given of everything. This is truly a clear favor." [17]Solomon's armies of jinn, men, and birds were brought before him and arranged in order. [18]When they came to the Valley of Ants, an ant said, "O ants! Go into your dwelling places before Solomon and his army unknowingly crush you." [19]He smiled and laughed at its words, saying, "Lord, help me to be thankful for the blessings you have bestowed on me and my parents, that I might do good words that please you. Include me among your righteous servants." (Q 27:16–19)

The reference to him being given a share of everything (v. 16) echoes the biblical story in 1 Kings 3 in which Solomon asks God for wisdom and is then provided with fame and treasure in addition to what he has requested. His prayer of thanksgiving at the end of the passage (v. 19) acknowledges his dependence on the deity and his submission to the divine will. The Bible does not mention the king's ability to communicate with animals, but the image of Solomon leading a large group of people, jinn, and birds resonates with the biblical presentation of him as a prominent political figure able to unite all of Israel under his authority. Solomon's ability to communicate with birds is most prominent in the story of his encounter with the Queen of Sheba, which in the Qur'an follows immediately after the passage above.

A Royal Visit

As with every woman mentioned in the text except Jesus's mother Mary, the Qur'an does not identify the Queen of Sheba by name. Other Islamic sources refer to her as Bilqis (*bilqīs*), and this is how many Muslims know her. Her visit to Solomon is described in chapter 27 of the Qur'an, and it differs from the biblical account in significant ways. What follows is an analysis of the passage divided into three sections and followed by a discussion of the relationship of the entire passage to the biblical story in 1 Kings 10:1–13, which appears in a nearly identical version in 2 Chronicles 9:1–12.

THE HOOPOE'S REPORT

[20]Solomon inspected the birds and said, "Why do I not see the hoopoe? Is it missing? [21]I will punish it harshly, or kill it, if it does not bring me an explanation." [22]The hoopoe was not gone long, and then said, "I have learned something you do not know, and I have come to you from Sheba with a reliable report. [23]I found a woman who has been given everything ruling over them, and she has a magnificent throne. [24]I found her and her people worshiping the sun rather than God. Satan has made their deeds seem appealing to them, and he has kept them from the right way so they are not properly guided. [25]They do not worship God, who brings out what is hidden in the heavens and on the earth and who knows what you conceal and what you reveal. [26]There is no god but God, Lord of the magnificent throne." (Q 27:20–26)

The hoopoe bird (*hudhud*) speaks nearly seventy words to Solomon's twenty in the Arabic text. The area of Sheba (*saba'*) was well known in antiquity as a land in southern Arabia through which much caravan traffic passed. The hoopoe reports that its Queen "has been given everything" (v. 23), and this phrase is virtually identical to what Solomon says about himself a few verses earlier (v. 16), so the implication is that they are equals in terms of the riches they possess. The reference to her luxurious throne might be a way of suggesting that she has something that even Solomon himself does not have.

When the bird faults her and her people for worshiping the sun instead of God, it implies that the queen does not recognize that the deity is the one behind her success. In this way, the passage demonstrates that nonhuman beings like the hoopoe can also be aware of God's power and submit to it. For instance, the bird states, "There is no god but God, Lord of the magnificent throne" (v. 26). The first half of that sentence contains an expression commonly found on the lips of Muslims, while the second half links God to the queen through the phrase "the mighty throne" (al- 'arsh al- 'aẓīm) while being somewhat ambiguous as to its precise point. Is the hoopoe saying that the deity is the one behind and responsible for the queen's magnificent throne, or is it claiming that only God's throne, not hers, is truly mighty? Whatever its exact meaning, the bird's words point the finger at the one who is commonly cited in the Qur'an as the source of human sin and shortcomings—Satan (v. 24).

TESTING—ROUND ONE

Solomon then sends the hoopoe bird back to the land of Sheba with a message for its queen. He does this in order to determine the bird's honesty, and in this way introduces the theme of testing that is an important part of the remainder of the story.

> [27]Solomon said, "We will see if you are telling the truth or lying. [28]Bring this letter of mine to them, and then withdraw to see what response they send." [29]She said, "O leaders, an honorable letter has been sent to me. [30]It is from Solomon and it states, 'In the name of God, the merciful and compassionate one, [31]do not place yourselves above me, but come to me in submission.'" [32]She

said, "O leaders, give me your advice on this matter since I do not decide on anything without your involvement." [33]They replied, "We are mighty and strong, but the matter is yours. So consider what your orders will be." [34]She said, "When kings enter a town they destroy it and make its most powerful people the weakest— this is what they do. [35]But I will send them a gift and then see what my messengers bring back." [36]The messenger came to Solomon and he [Solomon] said, "Are you trying to increase my wealth? What God has given to me is better than what He has given to you, but you are rejoicing over this gift of yours. [37]Go back to them! We will come upon them with armies they will not be able to confront, and we will expel them from there in humiliation and shame."

Solomon and the queen adopt a similar strategy by sending something to the other party in an attempt to bring them over to their own side, but each one's objective is not completely clear. Solomon is the more aggressive of the two with his command that the queen come to him in submission, while she tries to win him over by offering him gifts.

The letter from Solomon to the queen begins with the phrase, "in the name of God, the merciful and compassionate one," which is present throughout the Qur'an as a superscription or introduction for every chapter but one.[2] The statement is often referred to as the "basmala," which slightly adapts the sound of the first two words in its Arabic form (*bismi allāh al-rahmān al-rahīm*), and this is the only place it appears in the text of the Qur'an outside those superscriptions. Solomon's use of it to open his letter to the queen is a way of highlighting his piety as a prophet chosen by God. He goes on to urge her and her people to come to him in submission, and there is some ambiguity as to exactly what he is telling them to do (v. 31). Is Solomon ordering them to submit to himself or to God? The former reading can be supported by Solomon's threat that he and his forces will invade Sheba and completely overwhelm and embarrass its occupants (v. 37). Alternatively, the more theological reading is supported by what takes place at the end of the story, when the queen submits herself to the God of Solomon (v. 44).

The type of gift the queen sends to Solomon is not specified (v. 35), and it too can be interpreted as a test meant to determine his state of mind and level of aggression. The king's response is immediate and once again in line with his role as a prophet. He rejects her present as an attempt to buy him off by adding to his wealth, and then he boasts of all that God has given him that has rendered her gift meaningless and trivial (v. 36).

TESTING—ROUND TWO

[38]He (Solomon) said, "O leaders, which of you will bring me her throne before they come to me in submission?" [39]One of the jinn said, "I will bring it to you before you rise from your place. I am strong and can be trusted." [40]But one who had knowledge of the book said, "I can bring it to you in the twinkling of an eye." When Solomon saw it before him, he said, "This is a grace from my Lord, to test whether I am thankful or ungrateful. Whoever is thankful is thankful for his own sake, but if anyone is ungrateful, then my Lord is self-sufficient and generous." [41]He then said, "Disguise her throne for her, and we will see if she is rightly guided or not." [42]When she arrived, she was asked, "Is your throne like this one?" She said, "It looks like it." [Someone said], "We were given knowledge before her, and we submitted ourselves." [43]She had been prevented by what she worshipped that was not God, for she came from an unbelieving people. [44]It was said to her, "Enter the palace," but when she saw it she thought it was a pool of water and she bared her legs. Solomon said, "It is a palace paved with crystal." She cried out, "My Lord, I have wronged myself! With Solomon, I submit to God, the Lord of the Worlds."

The theme of testing continues in this section, as Solomon believes he is being tested by God when the queen's throne is placed before him (v. 40), and then she is twice tested by him when she is questioned about the throne and later is told to enter the hall with the glass floor (vv. 42–44). This suggests that a key issue of this story is whether or not these rulers are loyal servants of God. Words from the Arabic root *s-l-m*, from which the terms "Islam" and "Muslim" also come, appear three times in the section. In verse 38 Solomon announces that the queen and her party will be coming to him in submission (*muslimīn*), and as in its previous usage (v. 31), the term's meaning is not completely clear. It could be taken in the political sense that they are to submit to Solomon's authority as king, or in the theological sense that they should embrace monotheism and surrender to God's will. The same word appears a few verses later where the term is translated "submitted ourselves" (*muslimīn*; v. 42). It is unclear who speaks these words. Solomon could be talking about himself and his people, or the words could be spoken by someone in the queen's party. If the latter, then they are saying that they had become monotheists while she continued to be a polytheist. If so, she does not remain an unbeliever for long because the same Arabic root is found in the queen's final words of the section when she says, "I submit" (*aslamtu*), signifying her complete surrender to Solomon's God (v. 44).

The Queen of Sheba's double test is an interesting aspect of this story that does not have a parallel in the biblical tradition. Her throne is miraculously transported to Solomon by one of the jinn who is described by an Arabic term (*'ifrīt*) not translated here (v. 39). This is the only time it is found in the Qur'an, but outside the Islamic scripture it can carry a sense of evil or wickedness and it is sometimes used in reference to Satan. When she is questioned about it she says that it appears to be her throne, but it is unclear if she recognizes it as her own. The second test exposes more fully the queen's inability to properly identify her surroundings when she mistakes a room with a glass floor for a pool of water and exposes the lower portion of her legs to keep her clothing and shoes dry. Although she fails these tests, the queen ultimately earns a passing grade because she admits her errors and joins with Solomon in submitting to God by rejecting worship of the sun (v. 44).

INTERPRETATION OF SOLOMON AND THE QUEEN OF SHEBA

Some aspects of the Qur'an's presentation of Solomon have little direct connection to the biblical traditions about him. In the Bible he does not speak the language of birds or ants, nor does he have authority over the wind or other forces of nature. At the same time, some passages in the Qur'an clearly interpret biblical narratives. The most obvious similarity between the two portraits of Solomon is that both the Qur'an and the Bible call attention to his building activities and the many things he received from God. The Qur'an makes no mention of the wisdom of Solomon, which is a significant aspect of his character in the Bible. He is given knowledge in the Islamic text, but he is not directly associated with wisdom (Q 27:15). The Arabic term for knowledge in this verse (*'ilm*) should not be seen as a synonym for wisdom (*ḥikmah*). For instance, both are given to Moses in another passage and are considered separate qualities (Q 28:14). The Qur'an also states that God gave David wisdom (Q 38:20), and he is the only person in the Qur'an who directly receives wisdom from the deity.

The accounts of the Queen of Sheba's visit to Solomon are markedly different in the Qur'an and the Bible.[3] Solomon comes across as more pious in the Qur'an's story of the visit, as is evident in how he responds to the gifts the queen presents to him. According to 1 Kings, her entourage brought camels bearing spices, a great deal of gold, and precious stones when she came to Jerusalem (1 Kgs 10:2), and before she departed she gave him 120 talents of gold, a great quantity of spices, and precious stones (1 Kgs 10:10). The biblical narrative implies that the king accepted all of these gifts, but that is not how he responds to her largesse in the Qur'an. In the Islamic text, Solomon is insulted by what he considers to be an attempt to bribe him, and his rejection of the gifts is framed within the context of his relationship with God (Q 27:36). Perhaps this is an interpretive response to the biblical condemnation of Solomon for having his heart turned from God through his love of wealth, horses, and women. In any case, Solomon's display of piety is in keeping with his role as a prophet in Islam, since those who have been chosen by God are unwavering in their commitment to the deity. Another interesting difference between the two texts is that Solomon returns the favor in the Bible by presenting the queen with gifts, but he does not do this in the Qur'an (1 Kgs 10:13). As a prophet, the Islamic Solomon is interested only in converting her to belief in the one true God, not in honoring her with presents.

The testing theme also functions differently in the two versions of the story. The biblical account opens by stating that the queen came to test Solomon's wisdom (1 Kgs 10:1), and then he proceeds to answer all her questions, even though none of them are specified in the text (1 Kgs 10:3). In the Qur'an she does not test him, but he tests her several times through his letter and the episodes involving her throne and the glass floor. Solomon never tests the queen in the Bible. This difference likely reflects the varying purposes of the two stories. As in other sections of the biblical account of Solomon's reign,[4] the focus here is on the king's wisdom, as the queen makes direct reference to it several times (1 Kgs 10:4, 6–8). She tests him in order to confirm and verify the reports of his wisdom that she has heard, and Solomon passes the test without difficulty. In this way, the story of her visit legitimates Solomon's wisdom in the eyes of this wealthy foreign ruler.

The qur'anic story does not present Solomon as a wise and powerful king, but rather highlights his role as a prophet who facilitates the queen's conversion to belief in God. Her testing of him in the Bible confirms his status as a wise and wealthy ruler, while his testing of her in the Qur'an celebrates his status as a messenger who rejects the trappings of worldly possessions and helps bring another person to faith in the one God. In the biblical telling of the visit she blesses the God of Israel, but the focus is still clearly on Solomon (1 Kgs 10:9). Her final words in the Qur'an passage point to her new status as a believer who has now submitted herself to Solomon's God (Q 27:44b).

There is an intriguing similarity between the Islamic story and the Second Targum of Esther, an extracanonical Jewish text written in Aramaic that likely predates Islam. The targumic text describes Solomon sending the hoopoe bird, the Queen's visit to his palace after consulting her advisors, and her mistaken belief that the glass floor is water.[5] Much of that version of their encounter, like the one in the Qur'an, is set in the queen's land of Sheba, but the entirety of the biblical version takes place in Jerusalem where Solomon lives. Given these connections, it is likely that the targumic text served as a model or source for the Qur'an's account of the queen's visit to Solomon.

Further Biblical Interpretations

In the Hebrew Bible, both 1 Kings and 1–2 Chronicles include accounts of how Solomon became king upon the death of his father, David. As noted above, the Chronicler generally presents a sanitized version of events involving David and Solomon in comparison with its sources in the Deuteronomistic History, and that is the case here. By contrast, the description in 1 Kings is full of palace intrigue, deception, and bloodshed, as David's other son Adonijah (Solomon's half brother) claims the throne for himself, while the prophet Nathan and David's wife Bathsheba conspire to put her son Solomon on it (1 Kgs 1:5–53). According to 1 Chronicles, David's final words are in the form of a prayer to God (29:10–19), who has chosen Solomon as king, while in 1 Kings he resembles Don Vito Corleone in Mario Puzo's *The Godfather*: on his deathbed he has a father-son chat with Solomon in which he tells his son to kill all the family's enemies who have wronged David and pose a threat to Solomon's becoming king (1 Kgs 2:1–10). The Chronicler makes no mention of Adonijah's attempt to claim the throne or of the arrangement between Nathan and Bathsheba to convince David to make Solomon king. This type of reinterpretation of the events is commonplace in the Chronicler's account, which contains no details that might put David or Solomon in a negative light.

Solomon's attribute of wisdom finds a place in several biblical books that fit the genre of Wisdom literature, a type of writing found throughout the ancient Near East that offers reflections and observations about life that are based on common human experiences shared by all people. The Books of Job, Proverbs, and Qoheleth are the three examples of Wisdom Writings in the Hebrew Bible, and two of those three books have an association with Solomon.

The Book of Proverbs is a set of collections of proverbial sayings that circulated independently before they were gathered together. The first collection (chapters 1—9) begins with the words, "The proverbs of Solomon son of David, king of Israel" (Prov 1:1). The second collection (Prov 10:1—22:16) begins in a similar way—"The proverbs of Solomon" (Prov 10:1). In addition, the collection found in chapters 25 through 29 is identified as "other proverbs of Solomon that the officials of King Hezekiah of Judah copied" (Prov 25:1). The attribution of this material to Solomon reflects his association with wisdom elsewhere in the Bible, as discussed above. Scholars do not believe authorship of these texts can be traced back to Solomon, but those responsible for editing the collection identified them with him as a way of adding credibility and authority to their work.

The same thing can be seen in the Book of Qoheleth, which takes its name from the Hebrew term that the author uses to identify himself, which can mean "teacher" or "gatherer." The latter sense might be a reference to the great amount of wisdom or wealth the author accumulated during his lifetime.[6] In the first verse of the book, the author identifies himself as "the Teacher, the son of David, king in Jerusalem," and elsewhere in the first two chapters he continues to refer to his status as a ruler (Qoh 1:12; 2:12). Although Solomon is not mentioned by name in the book, several pieces of evidence suggest that the book was intended to be attributed to him. The author is referred to as the son of David in the opening verse, and Solomon was the only one of David's sons to become king. In addition, there are a number of references to the building projects the author undertook and the commercial transactions he engaged in, which fit with the description of Solomon's reign that is presented in 1 Kings (Qoh 2:4–8). Moreover, the author claims to be a very wise person (Qoh 2:9; cf. Qoh 1:13, 16–17; 2:12). As in the case of the Book of Proverbs, scholars do not believe that Solomon was the actual author of Qoheleth, which was likely written during the late Persian period, or perhaps later. Rather, he has been indirectly associated with it in order to give it more authority.

Song of Songs provides a final example of ancient attribution of a biblical work to Solomon. This book, also known as the Song of Solomon, is the Bible's only example of erotic poetry. The very first verse of the work establishes a connection with Solomon

("The Song of Songs, which is Solomon's"), but this superscription likely means the book is dedicated to him rather than that he is its author. Solomon is mentioned by name six other times in the text (Song 1:5; 3:7, 9, 11; 8:11–12), and a king is referred to in three other verses (Song 1:4, 12; 7:5). Yet in none of those passages does Solomon speak, and none of them would indicate that he wrote the book. The vocabulary and other literary evidence in the text suggest that it comes from a much later time than his, and it is likely that it has been associated with Solomon due to the comment in the description of his reign earlier in the Bible that he composed more than one thousand songs (1 Kgs 4:32). Thus, one of the main ways that the Bible interprets Solomon is by assigning him a role as the putative author of certain texts in order to endow them with his authority and prestige.

Solomon is referred to twice by Jesus, and each of those passages is found in the Gospels of both Matthew and Luke. In a teaching that instructs people not to be concerned about the clothing they wear, Jesus calls attention to the lilies of the field and says that even Solomon was not clothed in such majesty (Matt 6:28–29; Luke 11:27). In another place Jesus alludes to the Queen of Sheba's visit to Solomon to listen to his wisdom, and then goes on to claim that he is greater than Solomon (Matt 12:42; Luke 11:31). Each of these passages refers to one of Solomon's traditionally recognized characteristics in order to make a point. If Solomon's wealth and majesty were great, Jesus declares that they do not compare with what God will bestow on anyone who has faith. If Solomon's wisdom was great, it pales in comparison to what is revealed in Jesus through his life, death, and resurrection.

Focus for Comparison

The biblical and qur'anic interpretations of Solomon's life go in different directions. The Islamic Solomon has special powers like mastery over the wind and the ability to command animals and other nonhuman beings. This lends him the aura of a magician or wonder worker. In the Qur'an he also has the role of a prophet, one of only a select group of individuals who have had a unique relationship with God. The Qur'an uses these characteristics in

145

portraying Solomon as obediently submissive to God and also as effective in leading the Queen of Sheba to be likewise submissive. The Solomon of the Bible is associated with a skill set that centers on his wisdom and creativity, even as his disobedience to the "law of the king" is used to help explain the disaster of the Babylonian exile. As with his father, David, the retelling of his life story in Chronicles presents an image of Solomon that is exemplary and beyond reproach. He may not be a prophet in the Bible, but he possesses qualities that set him apart from other people. He is also a man who has a way with words. His reputation for wisdom led in antiquity to the attribution to Solomon of several biblical books that were written centuries after his death. His association with them played no small part in their being included in the canon.

Questions to Consider

1. What do you consider to be the most significant differences between how the Bible and the Qur'an present Solomon?

2. The Qur'an does not associate Solomon with wisdom, but is there anything in its description of him that suggests he was wise?

3. What is your reaction to the idea that Solomon had control over the wind and the jinn?

4. Is the theme of Solomon's submission to God's will present in the Bible like it is in the Qur'an?

5. In the Qur'an, is it more likely that Solomon is telling the Queen of Sheba to submit to himself or to God? What evidence might support your response?

6. How might the connections between the Second Targum of Esther and the Qur'an's account of the visit of the Queen of Sheba be explained?

7. What is your reaction to how the Solomon tradition is interpreted in other parts of the Bible?

CHAPTER 9

Job and Satan

Job is mentioned by name four times in the Qur'an, but only two of those passages relate directly to the biblical Book of Job (Q 21:83–84; 38:41–44). Of the other passages, one lists him as one of eighteen individuals who, because of their good works, have received favor and guidance from God through wisdom and status as a prophet (Q 6:83–90). Two chapters earlier, Job and most of the others mentioned in the first text are said to have received divine revelation (Q 4:163–65). Job is one of a number of biblical figures, like Lot, Aaron, and Zachariah, whom the Qur'an considers to be prophets, but who do not have that title in the Bible. In addition to this way of interpreting Job, the Qur'an includes two passages in which Job plays a more active role.

Job, the Reminder

The Qur'an treats Job in its twenty-first chapter, which carries the title "The Prophets" because its latter part contains stories about various individuals from the past, many of whom are recognized as prophets in Islam. It also includes a relatively brief section on Job that describes a set of circumstances that might be related to the biblical book about him:

> [83]Remember Job, when he cried to his Lord, "Indeed, hardship has come upon me. Suffering has truly afflicted me, but You are the most merciful of the merciful." [84]We

responded and took away his hardship, and We gave him back his family, and others like them, as a mercy from Us and a reminder for those who are servants. (Q 21:83–84)

COMPARISON WITH THE BIBLICAL NARRATIVE

This passage has five things in common with the biblical story of Job: (1) Job suffers; (2) he cries out in his pain; (3) his attitude shifts; (4) God responds; (5) God gives Job a new family. The text provides no narrative details, so we do not know the cause of Job's suffering, the form it took, how long it lasted, or precisely how God might have interacted with him. Nonetheless, this pattern of suffering followed by a lament from Job, Job's shift in attitude, a response from God, and Job's receiving of new family matches what takes place in the biblical book. The size of the biblical book—1,070 verses divided into 42 chapters—dwarfs this two-verse portion of the Qur'an. At the same time, only a fraction of the biblical text contains narrative, which occurs in two prose sections that frame the book (Job 1:1—2:13; 42:7–17).

The bulk of that narrative occurs in the thirty-five verses of the first two chapters, which describe how God and the Satan strike a deal to test the integrity of Job's faithfulness to God. Job is called "blameless and upright, one who feared God and turned away from evil" (Job 1:1), but the Satan proposes that God allow Job's property, family, and health to be taken from him to see if he is behaving blamelessly only in order to receive such blessings from God. The reader knows that Job's suffering does not result from his sin. Even after his animals, servants, and children have all been killed as a result of raids and natural disasters, Job engages in a set of mourning rituals and expresses his continued faith in God (Job 1:21). After the Satan causes him to break out in painful sores over his entire body, and Job's wife suggests that it would be better if he would blame God for his situation and die, Job continues to remain faithful (Job 2:7–10).

A coda in Job 42:7–17 explains how God gave Job new children and twice the amount of property that he had lost. In the nearly forty chapters of poetry between those two prose sections,

Job's attitude shifts first to angry protest and ultimately to reverent awe (Job 3:1—42:6). These chapters explore the question of suffering from a number of angles, including conversations between Job and his friends and a conversation between Job and God.

The Satan character in the biblical story should not be confused with the figure of Satan commonly equated with the devil. The latter is a relatively late development in Judaism, and by the time of Jesus, Satan was well established as the personification of evil. But prior to this, when the Book of Job was written, the concept of Satan as the devil had not yet been formed. The Hebrew word for Satan (*sāṭān*) can mean "accuser," "adversary," and "opponent," and in the Hebrew and Greek versions of this story it always appears as "the Satan," prefixed by the definite article and so suggesting a title rather than a personal name. English translations, however, tend to omit the definite article. Based on the way he is presented in the prose prologue (the Satan does not appear elsewhere in the book), he appears to be a member of the heavenly court who has the task of monitoring what is happening on earth and reporting to God about it.

INTERPRETATION OF JOB

Although Satan plays a role in the other Qur'an passage that mentions Job (treated below), he does not appear in this one. Here Job states that "hardship has come upon me," but the text does not mention the agreement between the Satan and God or any other cause of his pain. Unconcerned with either the cause of Job's suffering or his innocence, the text leaves no doubt as to how Job was freed of his anguish—God heard his cry, ended his suffering, and returned his family to him. The point is simple and straightforward, in sharp contrast to the detailed narrative frame and lengthy poetic speeches that compose the biblical book, which is one of the most difficult texts to interpret in the Hebrew Bible. While constraints of space do not allow a full overview of its themes here, two aspects of the interaction between Job and God emerge in contrast to the qur'anic version: the manner in which the two interact and the end result regarding Job's suffering. These differences reveal distinct theological purposes behind the two texts.

While the Qur'an portrays Job crying out to God in suffering, it does not elaborate on how he does this. The context of the Qur'an's overall emphasis on submission to God, however, suggests to the reader that Job petitioned God for help deferentially, that Job's suffering would not have moved him to question or protest against God. In short order, Job's attitude shifts from a cry of pain to an emphatic affirmation of God's mercy, in which he refers to God as "the most merciful of the merciful" (*arḥam al-rāḥimīn*). This is a distinctly Islamic way of describing the deity that highlights the important quality of mercy that is displayed throughout the Qur'an. The phrase is quite similar to the superscription that begins every chapter of the book but one and describes God as merciful and compassionate (*al-raḥmān al-raḥīm*). In the following verse, a different word from the same Arabic root is used to describe what God did for Job as "a mercy [*raḥmatan*] from Us." Job's words imply that God has the capacity to save him from his difficult situation because the deity is merciful, and the deity's use of a word that comes from the root that conveys mercy indicates that God has heard Job and has responded favorably to his request. Thus, the Islamic interpretation of Job highlights his trust in God's mercy, and because Job does not question God, God does not need to question Job.

The biblical story, by contrast, portrays a more complex way of relating to God, one that can include raw, honest expression of anger and protest as part of a process that can both be in tension with and facilitate trusting submission before the mystery of God. Moreover, while the Qur'an highlights God's mercy, the biblical text highlights God's mystery. Neither God's agreement to allow the Satan to inflict suffering on the innocent Job, nor God's speech to Job reflect an attitude of mercy. Rather, they challenge Job and the reader to reflect on God's mystery in light of inexplicable suffering. Job questions and protests against God in dramatic ways through interactions with his friends, who insist that his suffering must be punishment for some sin he has committed. As in the Qur'an, Job's attitude shifts, but in the biblical text this occurs only after expressions of not only pain, but also anger and protest move God to grant him the favor of a personal audience (38:1—42:6). God challenges Job through a set of rhetorical questions to recognize that there are mysteries beyond human comprehension, and Job responds with awe, acknowledging his lack of under-standing and disowning what he had said. After the dialogue with Job, God confronts the friends with a judgment in Job's favor, declaring that the friends were wrong to conclude that all suffering is deserved punishment for sin (42:7). Taken as a whole, the book validates a way of relating to God both with raw honesty—even including protest—and with openness to an encounter with the mystery of God that can transform one's perspective. Pointing to the centrality of actually encountering God, Job says, "I had heard of you by the hearing of the ear, but now my eye sees you" (Job 42:5). The book models the inherently dramatic character of what it means to relate to God in the Hebrew Bible, in which honest protest can lead to an encounter with God where awe transforms one's perspective, such that one's former words no longer ring true; but this does not mean it was wrong to utter them.[1]

The end result of the story in the Qur'an and the Bible is similar but not identical. The Qur'an says that Job's family is given back to him and that he also receives new family ("others like them"), while in the biblical narrative Job does not receive back his dead children but only new ones. Moreover, the Bible does not say that God removed Job's suffering. The biblical Job would have experienced some comfort and solace in the restoration of his property and in receiving new children, but can one replace chil-dren? In the biblical text, that Job—who is declared innocent from the start—is not freed of suffering serves the purpose of the book to prompt readers to imagine relating to God honestly and with openness to mystery, even in the midst of suffering, and even when that suffering seems unfair. That Job arrives at a new perspective on the mystery of God, and that God affirms Job's righteousness, restores his possessions, and grants him new children all combine to dramatize a fundamental affirmation of his way of proceeding in relating to God.

In the Qur'an Job's family is actually restored and so, if the Qur'an reflects the tradition in which Job's children had died, this fact is not clear from the text. Muslim scholars understand the reference to restoring Job's family in different ways. Some have argued that they were brought back to life after having died, oth-ers interpret it as saying that Job's family was returned to him after they had been away somewhere, and still others suggest that his family's restoration took the form of being healed in the water after they had bathed. Affirming that Job's family was restored complements the Qur'an's report that God removed Job's suffering. Job's uncomplicated shift from crying out in pain to affirming God's mercy makes him a model of trust and submission to God. In keeping with the Islamic view of the deity, God responds mercifully to Job's appeal, and Job receives back the same family that had been taken from him. The passage concludes with the statement that Job is a reminder for all God's servants, and this is why he is found in the company of all the other prophets who are mentioned in this chapter of the Qur'an.

Job, the Patient

A qur'anic passage that has more narrative structure than the one just discussed provides additional information about Job.

> [41]Remember Our servant Job, who cried out to his Lord, "Satan has afflicted me with fatigue and great pain." [42]"Stomp your foot! Here is a cool bath and drink." [43]We gave back to him his family, and others like them, as a mercy from Us and a reminder for those who possess reason. [44]"Take a small bunch of grass in your hand and strike with it so you do not break your oath." We found him to be patient in adversity and an excellent servant. He was always repentant. (Q 38:41–44)

COMPARISON WITH THE BIBLICAL NARRATIVE

An interesting element that this passage shares with the biblical Book of Job is that both refer to him as God's "servant" (vv. 41, 44; Job 1:8; 2:3). Many prophets are described in this way in the Qur'an because being a servant requires that one adopt the position of submission and surrender that is at the heart of the message of Islam. This is precisely how Job responds in the prose portion of the biblical text when he accepts the suffering and misfortune that come his way (Job 1:20–22; 2:9–10). The reference to Job crying out (v. 41), which is also found in the previous Qur'an passage, is another link with the biblical book. Here, however, Job identifies Satan as the cause of his affliction linking this passage to the biblical Book of Job, where the Satan plays a prominent role in Job's suffering. However, unlike the biblical text, which uses "the Satan," the Qur'an refers to the character simply as Satan, the devil. In both of these Qur'an passages Job receives back his family and others like them, while in the biblical text he receives new family.

Several elements in this Qur'an text have no equivalents in the Bible: (1) Job is told to stomp his foot (v. 42); (2) he is given water to drink from and bathe in (v. 42); (3) he is ordered to strike at someone or something with a bunch of grass (v. 44); and (4) reference is made to an oath that Job has made (v. 44). The first two are best seen as linked in a cause-and-effect relationship, as the stomping of Job's foot is what causes the water to miraculously appear. Many Muslim commentators interpret this as a reference to two different springs or small bodies of water, one of which serves as a bath that soothes his body and heals his wounds while the other allows him to quench his thirst. If this interpretation is adopted, this is the Qur'an's only (indirect) mention of the sores that cover Job's body in the Bible (Job 2:7–8). The identity of the speaker in verse 42 who instructs Job to stomp his foot and then drink and bathe is not explicitly stated, but the wider literary context indicates that it is God, since the verse is immediately followed by another in which the deity's role in restoring Job back to his former status is highlighted. This verse uses the same word (*raḥmatan*) found in the previous passage that highlights the key qur'anic theme of God's mercy (v. 43; cf. Q 21:84).

The first part of verse 44 has been a focus of scholarly debate because of its difficulty, as it is unclear exactly what Job is told to do. One point of unclarity is that the passage does not indicate who or what Job is supposed to hit with the grass. The Arabic words translate into English simply as "and strike with it." Another problem concerns the reference to Job's oath that follows the order for him to strike. The details of the oath are not expressed in the verse, and such an oath is not referred to in any other Qur'an passage that mentions Job.

INTERPRETATION OF JOB

Many read the command to strike and the oath Job makes as somehow related, maintaining that he is being told to strike because of some oath he has taken. This interpretation sees an implicit reference to Job's wife, who is otherwise not mentioned in the Qur'an. According to some commentators, Job had vowed to punish his wife because she had listened to Satan, and so in this verse God tells him that he can strike her lightly with a handful of grass that will inflict no pain on her. Variations on this interpretation say that he swore to strike her one hundred times for a variety of different reasons, including her lack of concern about his situation and her selling one of her braids in order to feed him.[2] According to some, after Job became well again God ordered him to reduce the severity of the oath and told him to strike her once with one hundred blades of grass or twigs. The origin of the tradition about the oath is unknown because it does not appear in the hadith collections that record the sayings of the Prophet Muhammad or in the collections known as Stories of the Prophets that relate events in the lives of earlier prophetic figures. Perhaps Muslim commentators introduced Job's wife into the passage because they were aware of her role in the biblical story. However her presence might be explained and whatever Job's oath might have entailed, this is a good example of how the Qur'an's lack of narrative detail can create challenges for its readers and commentators.[3]

Job's identification of only Satan as responsible for his afflictions—without implicating God in any way—points to a major difference between how this Qur'an passage and the biblical book interpret Job. In the latter text, while the Satan is the direct cause of Job's suffering, he can play this role only because God allows it. The first two chapters make clear that the Satan is the direct agent responsible for all of Job's suffering, but two conversations between the Satan and God establish that God allows the series of catastrophes that befall Job (Job 1:7–12; 2:2–6). Job is unaware of the Satan's involvement or the arrangement worked out with God that lead to Job's misfortune, as is evident from his statements that the Lord has given and can take away, and that we must receive both good and bad from God's hand. For theological purposes, framing Job's suffering in this way raises both problems and possibilities.

The opening verses of the biblical book describe Job in two ways. First, he is a good man. He is blameless, in proper relationship with God, and he turns away from evil. Second, he is exceedingly prosperous. In both family and material wealth he is "the greatest of all the people of the east" (Job 1:1–5). The Satan's plan serves as an experiment intended to test Job by making him suffer in order to see if his righteous behavior and respect for God are contingent on obtaining good things from God, or if they are unconditional. Is Job's proper behavior self-serving, or does his dedication to God and to upright living stem fundamentally from faithfulness to God?

There are problems: If God knows that Job is an honorable man and a faithful servant, why then does God allow the Satan to torture him? No one would dare propose this sort of experiment in any research institute since it would be considered extremely unethical. The same might be asked regarding Job's children, servants, and animals, who are nothing but collateral damage in a contest between God and the Satan meant to determine Job's true character. Yet there are possibilities. In the context of the book, this narrative frame sets up the speeches that follow and so allows the book to confront the limitations of the assumption commonly held in the ancient Near East, as in many cultures, that somehow life is basically fair, that good behavior brings rewards and evil behavior brings suffering.

One can see Job to represent those who lead good lives and avoid doing wrong, and yet are confronted with pain and suffering that they do not believe they deserve. In this respect, one could see the Book of Job responding to the so-called question of theodicy, which asks how God can be both all good and all powerful, while at the same time allowing innocent people to suffer. This way of posing the problem of suffering seeks an answer in terms of propositional logic; it wants a clear, linear explanation. To the extent that this sort of answer is proposed in the Book of Job, as in the friends' speeches, it is rejected by God (42:7). For the biblical book, the question of suffering can be addressed in a process of expressing honest anger and protest while maintaining openness to being transformed in the mysterious presence of God. Moreover, the lengthy speeches in which Job voices angry protest do not reflect only his own experience in the first two chapters, but they treat human suffering more expansively and so invite readers to reflect not only on "innocent suffering" but also on the ordinary suffering of their lives. The biblical book emphasizes that the existence of suffering will remain a mystery that eludes human understanding. It portrays the relationship between God and Job as unfolding through a messy process in which God expresses care for Job not by promising to protect him from harm, but by allowing him a personal encounter that Job ultimately finds satisfying, even though Job has to face his own smallness within the cosmos of God's creation.

The questions raised above regarding God's allowing the Satan to inflict suffering on Job would present significant problems from the qur'anic perspective because they directly challenge the Islamic understanding of the deity. The notion that God would cause suffering on an innocent person who obediently submits to the divine will is diametrically opposed to the Qur'an's view of the divine-human relationship, which is dominated by the concept of mercy. Similarly, the idea that God might be manipulated to enter into a bargain with a figure like Satan that would result in torment for a faithful servant would go completely against the Islamic understanding of the deity as the supreme authority who has compassion on all of creation.

The Qur'an interprets the Job tradition so that it better reflects Muslim theology and belief. It distances God from Job's suffering by identifying Satan as the one responsible for it. It describes the deity extending mercy toward Job by providing him with water to quench his thirst and soothe his pain, and it explains how God restores Job's family to him. Similarly, there is no arrangement between the deity and Satan that causes Job undue hardship and compromises God's power and authority. In both the Qur'an and the Bible Job remains steadfast and faithful despite his troubles, but the Islamic text makes it clear that God is not the source or cause of those troubles, and it does not portray Job protesting angrily against God, because God is not considered responsible for his suffering.

It is surprising that Job does not play a bigger role in the Qur'an, because he might be the biblical figure who best personifies the tenets of Islam. One might wonder whether familiarity with biblical traditions in which Job protests against God might be responsible for his relatively small role in the Qur'an. Yet, as presented there, he suffers indescribable pain through the loss of his children and possessions, in addition to the physical agony he must endure. Despite all that hardship, he responds as an ideal Muslim by surrendering and submitting himself to the divine will, and in the end he is rewarded. Even though he is mentioned only a few times in the text, the Qur'an holds him up as an example to be followed: "Remember Our servant Job" (Q 38:41). It celebrates his patience and ability to remain faithful in the midst of his suffering: "We found him to be patient in adversity and an excellent servant. He was always repentant" (Q 38:44).

Further Biblical Interpretations

The only other book of the Hebrew Bible that mentions Job is Ezekiel, which does so in a passage discussed above in chapter 4 concerning Noah. While the writer of Ezekiel was familiar with traditions about Job, the relationship between whatever traditions the writer possessed and the biblical Book of Job remains unclear. In a message from God to the prophet, a series of hypothetical scenarios name Noah, Daniel, and Job as righteous individuals who lived long ago (Ezek 14:12–20). Each scenario imagines a land that God might somehow punish, and each concludes by stating that if Noah, Daniel, and Job were living in that land they would be able to save only themselves.

Ezekiel's interest in Job has simply to do with his righteousness, an issue at the core of the Book of Job. As discussed in chapter 4, Ezekiel uses Job and the other two ancient heroes to make the point that people's righteousness benefits themselves.[4] This point supports Ezekiel's message intended to encourage the survivors of the Babylonian destruction of Jerusalem and subsequent exile. Lest they see themselves as powerless victims of a punishment brought upon them by the misdeeds of their ancestors, Ezekiel sought to reinforce belief that their own actions matter (cf. Ezek 18:21–23). By emphasizing the simple link between right behavior and reward, Ezekiel conveys a different message than the more complex meditation on suffering found in Job.

The Letter of James is the only New Testament writing that mentions Job by name. In a section that urges its readers to endure despite their hardships and difficulties, the author cites Job as a model they might follow.

> [8]You also must be patient. Strengthen your hearts, for the coming of the Lord is near. [9]Beloved, do not grumble against one another, so that you may not be judged. See, the Judge is standing at the doors! [10]As an example of suffering and patience, beloved, take the prophets who spoke in the name of the Lord. [11]Indeed we call blessed those who showed endurance. You have heard of the endurance of Job, and you have seen the purpose of the Lord, how the Lord is compassionate and merciful. (Jas 5:8–11)

Job is cited here as the quintessential patient person because he remained faithful despite his hardships. As noted above, this resembles the way he functions in the Qur'an as an example that should be emulated. Yet the image of Job as a submissive and silent sufferer is at odds with how he is presented in the biblical book, given how in the poetic section he complains that he has been treated wrongfully and demands a hearing with God so he might plead his case. Only in the prose prologue and epilogue does Job passively accept his situation.

The author of James also interprets Job by giving him a title he does not possess in the Hebrew Bible. After advising its audience to take the prophets as examples (v. 10), the letter then immediately mentions Job (v. 11). This creates the impression that Job is to be counted among the prophets, but nowhere in the Book of Job is he described in this way. By suggesting that Job is a prophet, the Letter of James resonates with the Qur'an, which considers Job a prophet. The final words of this passage from James, which describe the Lord as merciful and compassionate, provide another noteworthy, if coincidental, link to the Qur'an. These are the adjectives most commonly used to refer to God in Islam, and they echo the words of Job himself in the Qur'an when he says, "You are the most merciful of the merciful" (Q 21:83).

Focus for Comparison

Of the passages from Ezekiel and James, neither offers a significant or dramatic interpretation of the Job tradition, but what they have in common is worth noting. Each points to Job as one who embodies a virtue—in Ezekiel it is his righteousness, while James calls attention to his patient endurance as a model for others. Job functions as an exemplar in the Islamic text as well, so in this way he serves as a reminder for both those who read the Bible and those who read the Qur'an. All of these interpretations of Job demonstrate marked contrast with the manner in which the Book of Job explores the mystery of suffering by engaging God in a process that can include angry protest before it reaches an awe-inspiring and transformative encounter with God.

Questions to Consider

1. Which are more significant for you, the similarities or the differences in how Job is presented in the Bible and the Qur'an?

2. How is Job's relationship with God in the Qur'an similar to and different from the way it is presented in the Bible?

3. What is your reaction to the different ways the Satan figure functions in the Qur'an and the Bible?

4. Is Job presented in a more positive light in the Qur'an than he is in the Bible? Why or why not?

5. What in the biblical text might suggest that there is anything merciful about God's words and actions in the Book of Job?

6. Does either the Bible or the Qur'an do a better job of exploring the mystery of suffering? What is the textual evidence for your choice?

7. Do you find it unusual that the author of the Letter of James refers to Job as a prophet?

CHAPTER 10

Jonah and the Fish

The Qur'an mentions Jonah by name five times and also refers to him as "the one of the great fish" (*dhu al-nūn*) and "the companion of the fish" (*ṣaḥib al-ḥūt*). At four chapters, the biblical narrative of Jonah is not lengthy, but it provides much more information about the prophet than do the sixteen Qur'an verses that discuss him. In the biblical account, Jonah is sent to the city of Nineveh. Located near present-day Mosul, Nineveh was well known in ancient Israel as the last capital of the Assyrian Empire and was destroyed in 612 BCE by the Babylonians. The Assyrians had brought massive destruction upon the Israelites in the late eighth century BCE and continued to subjugate them long into the seventh century BCE. In the story, Jonah is sent to warn the Ninevites of their impending destruction, should they not change their evil ways. However, to Jonah's surprise they do so and God does not destroy them.

A verse in the Qur'an reflects this same pattern of repentance followed by divine mercy: "Why has no town believed in a way that its belief benefited it except for the people of Jonah? When they believed, We removed from them the punishment of humiliation in the life of this world and We granted them enjoyment for a while" (Q 10:98). Two differences from the biblical story are striking in this Qur'an passage. The people who repented remain anonymous in the Qur'an, whereas the Bible identifies them as Ninevites. In addition, the Islamic text refers to them as "Jonah's people," but this designation would not fit the biblical story because Jonah is not from Nineveh, and he adopts a hostile attitude toward the city and its residents. It is unclear in the Qur'an if the people to whom Jonah was sent were his own, as is typical in the Islamic text, or if he had no prior relationship with them. Before turning to the qur'anic text that has the most in common with the biblical Jonah story (Q 37:139–48), we first consider a couple of others about Jonah that demonstrate how the Islamic text has interpreted the biblical narrative.

The Man of the Fish (Q 21:87–88)

A brief Qur'an passage appears to be related to a famous episode recorded in the biblical Book of Jonah: "Remember the one of the great fish [*dhu al-nūn*], Jonah, when he angrily departed and thought We had no power over him. Then he cried out in the darkness, 'There is no God but You, glory to You! I have been one of the evildoers.' We responded and saved him from trouble. That is how We rescue those who believe" (Q 21:87–88).

COMPARISON WITH THE BIBLICAL NARRATIVE

These verses likely refer to the biblical scene in which God sends a great fish that swallows Jonah after he is cast into the sea by crew members of the boat he has boarded in an attempt to refuse God's call to go to Nineveh (Jonah 1:11–17). The Bible reports that Jonah spent three days inside the fish. The Qur'an passage does not explicitly state that Jonah is inside a fish, but the reference to his crying out "in the darkness" certainly fits with the location of the biblical Jonah. The fact that he utters a prayer while in the darkness as he does while within the fish in the Bible (Jonah 2) also supports this interpretation.

Although they both seek deliverance from his situation, the prayers Jonah recites in the Bible and the Qur'an are different in some important ways. The one in the Islamic text is much briefer. Its Arabic form contains only nine words, while the Hebrew text of the biblical prayer (Jonah 2:2–9) is nearly nine times as long. The tone and content of the two prayers also vary significantly.

161

Most notably, the Islamic Jonah does something that his biblical character does not do—he admits he has made a mistake when he says, "I have been one of the evildoers." When speaking with the sailors on the ship, Jonah acknowledges his responsibility for the storm that threatens to sink them (Jonah 1:12), but in the biblical prayer in which Jonah describes the predicament he is in and asks for God's assistance, he never acknowledges that he is the one responsible for his situation. Because the content of the biblical prayer does not fit its narrative context, many scholars have suggested that it might not have been a part of the original Jonah story but was added to it at a later point in time.[1]

Prior to admitting his mistake, the qur'anic Jonah begins his prayer with words that acknowledge God's uniqueness and majesty when he proclaims, "There is no God but You, glory to You!" (Q 21:87). The biblical Jonah does not do this, and the closest he comes to praising the deity is when he concludes his prayer with the words, "Deliverance belongs to the Lord!" (Jonah 2:9). But that statement is as much about Jonah as it is about God because the prophet is appealing to the deity with his own best interests in mind, as he wishes to be saved from his difficult circumstances. Much of the biblical Jonah's prayer expresses his self-interest, while the Islamic Jonah first acknowledges God's authority and might without asking anything for himself, and his only self-referential comment recognizes his own guilt. The prayer in the Qur'an also strongly echoes the first part of the Islamic profession of faith, which begins, "There is no God but God." In addition, the phrase "glory to You" (*subḥānaka*) that he utters is often found in Islamic prayer and ritual, so the passage presents Jonah as a pious individual whose devotion is very much in line with that of a typical Muslim.

INTERPRETATION OF JONAH

Despite that characterization, some aspects of the passage have raised questions for Qur'an commentators about Jonah. For instance, he did not behave as a prophet should when he went off angrily (*mughāḍiban*). This may reflect the opening scene in the biblical book, when Jonah refuses to heed God's call to go to Nineveh and instead attempts to flee to Tarshish (Jonah 1:1–3).

The reference to his anger sets Jonah apart from all the other prophets mentioned in the Qur'an, and commentators have tried to explain it in ways that suggest he was not angry at God but at something or someone else. These interpretations have no support in the Qur'an, but they are motivated by two factors—the lack of detail in the text and the desire to explain Jonah's anger in a way that aligns him with the Islamic view of prophecy.

Another issue that Muslim commentators have wrestled with in this passage concerns the mention that Jonah thought God had no power over him (Q 21:87). This verse could be read as stating that Jonah had doubts about God's authority and omnipotence, something that would go against the Qur'an's understanding of how prophets interact with the deity. Scholars have addressed this matter in a couple different ways. Some propose that one read the statement as a query that asks, "Did he think We could not restrict him?" Read in this way, it functions as a rhetorical question that highlights the absurdity of a person believing that God does not have control over his or her life. This proposal would solve the problem, but it is not supported by the grammar of the passage. The Arabic language marks questions with an interrogative particle, which is absent in this passage indicating that it is a statement and not a question. Another approach is to understand the Arabic verb translated here "to have power" (*qadara*) in a way that focuses not on God's power in general but on the way that power is exercised. In other words, Jonah acknowledged God's power, but he did not expect it to be used by imprisoning him in a fish.

The actions of the biblical Jonah, by contrast, call into question the extent of God's control over his life. When he first receives the commission to go to Nineveh, he thinks he can escape the deity by fleeing to a distant land. The story leaves no doubt that this is his intent because it states twice in the same verse that Jonah was going to Tarshish "away from the presence of the LORD" (Jonah 1:3). His escape plan is soon foiled, but when he goes to Nineveh after being called a second time (Jonah 3:1–5), he remains a petulant prophet throughout the remainder of the book. When God relents from punishing the Ninevites after they repent from their evil ways, Jonah is upset with this outcome, and this show of divine forgiveness leads him to say three times that he would rather be dead (Jonah 4:1–9). Therefore, two aspects that are central to the

Muslim view of the deity—God's authority and boundless mercy—are the very things the biblical Jonah most resents and resists. The Jonah of the Qur'an, though, recognizes that authority ("There is no God but You") and is a recipient of that mercy ("We responded and saved him from trouble"). According to this passage, the qur'anic Jonah possesses some flaws, but his prayer in distress helps to rehabilitate him and make him a model for those in a similar situation, who are in need of divine compassion.

Be Patient

In a passage addressed to the Prophet Muhammad, the Qur'an refers to Jonah not by name but by one of his titles:

> ⁴⁸Be patient for your Lord's judgment. Do not be like the companion of the fish [ṣaḥib al-ḥūt] when in distress he called out. ⁴⁹If favor from his Lord had not come to him, he would have been abandoned guilty on the shore. ⁵⁰But his Lord chose him and made him one of the righteous ones. (Q 68:48–50)

By recalling that Jonah cried out in anguish and received God's mercy, these verses appear to refer to the same episode as the previous passage, but the content of his prayer is not given as in the other text. The reference to Jonah calling out uses the same Arabic verb (nādā) that is in the previous passage, but this one also does not explicitly mention Jonah's anger or identify what he has done wrong, nor does Jonah acknowledge his guilt in it. Nonetheless, the passage has the same movement from pain to prayer to mercy that appears in the other one.

While the passage seems to situate Jonah as having been rescued from the fish, the passage is less concerned with the situation than to teach about God's mercy. By attributing to Jonah the title "companion of the fish" (ṣaḥib al-ḥūt) and specifying his being on a shore, this passage suggests that Jonah was inside a fish when he cried out. The Arabic word for that location ('ara'ā) comes from a root whose main meaning relates to nakedness, and it describes any open, barren, or desolate area. The passage appears to be describing the moment in the Bible when the fish spews Jonah onto dry land before the prophet receives the second commission to go to Nineveh (Jonah 2:10). The main point being made is that Jonah would have been despised and reviled by others if it had not been for God's choice of him that enabled him to be transformed into a blameless and upright person.

The most notable way in which this text interprets the Jonah tradition concerns the identity of its addressee. As seen in other passages, the Qur'an here cites an event in the life of a prophetic figure of the past to communicate a message or teaching to Muhammad. The opening part of the passage instructs the prophet of Islam to exercise patience (Q 68:48), a trait that was lacking in his predecessor Jonah. The Qur'an employs more than one hundred times the term (*ṣabr*) translated "be patient" here, which can also convey notions of endurance and perseverance.[2] Muhammad is to have patience in waiting for God's judgment, and the instruction implies that—but does not make explicit in what manner—Jonah lacked patience. The immediate reference to Jonah's calling out may suggest that he was impatient waiting to be rescued (v. 48). Moreover, if his rescue was understood to express God's judgment in his favor, a stronger link between the two characters emerges since the text also understands that Muhammad was awaiting God's judgment against enemies who were causing him distress: as God's judgment freed Jonah from distress, it would free Muhammad from his enemies.

In any case, to focus on Jonah's (im)patience would be to miss the main point of this Qur'an passage, which is really about Muhammad. The figure of Jonah, like many of Muhammad's other prophetic forebears mentioned in the Qur'an, serves as a mirror that allows him to reflect on his own life's circumstances. Muhammad is instructed to learn from the earlier prophet so he can avoid the mistakes Jonah made. Specifically, the passage urges him to exercise patience and perseverance in the face of the persecution and hostility he was experiencing from his contemporaries in Mecca, who refused to accept the monotheistic message he had brought them. This becomes clear in the two verses that follow the passage and conclude this chapter of the Qur'an. "The unbelievers practically trip you up with their looks when they hear the Qur'an and say, 'He is truly mad.' But it [the Qur'an] is nothing but a reminder for all" (Q 68:51–52). The opening words of the Jonah section ask Muhammad to be patient for his Lord's judgment, and these closing words of the chapter tell him that divine judgment will be directed against his detractors and he will ultimately be vindicated. If Muhammad calls out to God in his distress like Jonah did, he will be chosen and made one of the righteous ones.

The Man and the Fish

The Qur'an passage that has the most in common with the biblical Jonah story occurs in chapter 37 (vv. 139–48). Like the passages already treated, this one assumes familiarity with the biblical narrative and so is much briefer than that narrative and lacks many of its details.

> [139]Jonah was one of the messengers. [140]When he fled to the laden ship, [141]he cast lots and was the loser. [142]A great fish swallowed him, for he was to blame. [143] Had he not been one of those who glorify God, [144]he would have remained in its belly until the Day when all are raised up. [145]But We cast him out onto the shore while he was sick, [146]and We caused a gourd tree to grow over him. [147]We sent him to a hundred thousand (people) or more [148]and they believed, so We let them enjoy life for a while. (Q 37:139–48)

COMPARISON WITH THE BIBLICAL NARRATIVE

This Qur'an passage closely parallels the biblical narrative, having several key events in common with it.

1. Jonah flees to a ship. (Q 37:140; Jonah 1:3)
2. Lots are cast and Jonah is singled out. (Q 37:141; Jonah 1:7)
3. Jonah is swallowed by a fish. (Q 37:142; Jonah 1:17)

4. God casts Jonah out of the fish. (Q 37:145; Jonah 2:10)
5. God causes vegetation to grow over Jonah. (Q 37:146; Jonah 4:6)
6. More than one hundred thousand people live in the city. (Q 37:147; Jonah 4:11)
7. The people in the city become believers. (Q 37:148; Jonah 3:5)

Some portions of the biblical story do not have equivalents in the Qur'an. The Qur'an refers to Jonah as a messenger (v. 139), but it does not describe God sending Jonah to speak to the people. The biblical book, on the other hand, has the deity commission Jonah twice to go to the Ninevites and deliver a message to them (Jonah 1:1–2; 3:1–2). After Jonah refuses the first commission, God sends a storm that threatens the ship, and its crew members cast lots to determine who is responsible for the danger they are in. This storm is not mentioned in the Qur'an. Virtually the entire second chapter of the biblical book quotes a prayer that Jonah utters while inside the fish (Jonah 2:2–9). The two Qur'an passages discussed above refer to Jonah crying out in distress but only one of them includes his words, which are much fewer than they are in the Bible. The Qur'an does not contain the biblical scene in which the king of Nineveh repents in sackcloth and ashes and then issues a decree for his subjects to do the same. All the city's inhabitants, including their animals, obey his command and are saved (Jonah 3:6–9). In addition, the fourth chapter of the biblical book reports a conversation—not found in the Qur'an—between Jonah and God in which Jonah voices his displeasure at the saving of Nineveh and expresses three times his desire to die. Some of these differences contain important clues about how the Islamic text has interpreted the biblical one.

The final three verses of the Qur'an passage raise interesting issues about the chronological order of the events described (vv. 146–48). According to the biblical story, God provides the bush for Jonah after he has been sent to Nineveh and its residents have repented. But if we read the Qur'an passage sequentially, the order is reversed because the mention of Jonah being sent comes after God makes the gourd tree grow over him. Alternatively, it is possible to read the final verses as a summary of what has already taken place rather than a sequential account, and that way the biblical and qur'anic chronologies match up. Nonetheless, many Muslim commentators have opted to read the passage sequentially and therefore have a somewhat different understanding of how the events unfolded over time than what the Bible presents.

INTERPRETATION OF JONAH

The Qur'an typically emphasizes the message or point of the story rather than its plot, and this tendency accounts for the lack of narrative detail in the presentation of Jonah here. Moreover, the role that Jonah plays in the Qur'an and its lack of description of his resistance to God or his anger over God's decision to spare the people makes sense in light of the Qur'an's consistent portrayal of God's prophets in a positive light. The first verse of the passage describes Jonah as a messenger (*rasūl*), a lofty title found more than three hundred times in the Qur'an that describes a human emissary sent by God to deliver a message to a particular people. According to the Qur'an, every people has been given their own messenger: "We have sent a messenger to every people, saying, 'Worship God and avoid worshipping other gods.' Among them were some who were guided by God, but others were controlled by error. Go throughout the earth and see what happened to those who denied the truth" (Q 16:36; cf. Q 10:47).

While situating Jonah among those peoples who responded favorably to their messenger, the Qur'an does not quote any of the message that he delivered to them. Perhaps one reason for that absence is that, according to the biblical account, Jonah was a reluctant prophet at best. When God first called him, the instructions were quite clear: "Now the word of the LORD came to Jonah son of Amittai, saying, 'Go at once to Nineveh, that great city, and cry out against it; for their wickedness has come up before me'" (Jonah 1:1–2). But Jonah did not obey that command and decided to go in the opposite direction toward Tarshish (Jonah 1:3).[3] Jonah is called again in the Bible in words similar to those used the first time, and on this occasion he does go to Nineveh (Jonah 3:1–3). But after the people of the city respond favorably to his message by mending their ways and God shows them mercy,

Jonah is upset (Jonah 3:10–4:1). Jonah enjoys more success than any other prophet in the Bible, and yet he becomes angry because he does not think the people to whom he has been sent deserve to be spared punishment. As Nineveh was the last capital of the Assyrian empire, the biblical Jonah's anger over God's display of mercy may well reflect anger among the story's ancient Israelite audience at the Assyrian empire for the vast devastation and subjugation it had inflicted on Israel.

This response of Jonah is not appropriate for a prophet or messenger according to the Qur'an, which downplays the biblical tradition of Jonah as a reluctant prophet who has to be called twice, but it retains traces of it. The reference to Jonah's being blameworthy (v. 142) is likely an allusion to his attempted escape, as is the comment that he fled to the ship (v. 140). The Qur'an's description of the ship as overloaded is likely a way of identifying it as a commercial vessel like the one in the biblical story (Jonah 1:3–5). The Qur'an does not state specifically that Jonah fled from God's call, but someone familiar with the biblical tradition can read between the lines and know that the Islamic text is subtly alluding to his attempted escape.

According to the biblical story, the arrival of the fish was due to supernatural intervention (Jonah 1:17). Without mentioning the deity's involvement, the Qur'an simply says that a great fish swallowed Jonah because of what he did. This highlights an interesting difference between the two passages. In the Bible the fish is sent by God as a means of saving Jonah, but in the Qur'an it could be read as a form of punishment for the offenses he has committed even though Muslim scholars have usually not understood it that way. Interestingly, the Bible and the Qur'an agree that God is the one responsible for the fish depositing Jonah back on dry land (Q 37:145; Jonah 2:10).[4] In several places in the Qur'an God sends another creature to a person for assistance or to teach a lesson. As discussed in chapter 3, when one of the unnamed sons of Adam and Eve (Cain and Abel in the Bible) kills the other, God sends a bird to scratch on the ground and show him how he should bury his dead brother's corpse (Q 5:31).

In the biblical account Jonah sits down east of the city to see what will happen to it, and he builds a booth that provides him with shade (Jonah 4:5). God then gives the prophet additional cover by appointing a bush to grow over him (Jonah 4:6).[5] This is similar to the gourd tree that God makes come over Jonah in the Qur'an (v. 146). However, the next day God appoints a worm to destroy the bush and then sends a hot east wind that adds to Jonah's misery as he bakes in the sun (Jonah 4:7–8). These divine actions inflict punishment on Jonah and, combined with Jonah's triple declaration that he would rather be dead, point to the worsening relationship between God and the prophet. None of these events are recorded in the Qur'an, perhaps because they go against the Islamic belief that God does not do anything to harm a prophet. The same might be said about the image of the deity sending a large fish to swallow Jonah; since it could be seen as an instance of God possibly punishing or mistreating a prophet, this idea is downplayed in the Qur'an.

In general, the Qur'an interprets Jonah by presenting him in a more positive light than does the Bible. This passage calls attention to the way Jonah glorified God and was as a result not consigned to the belly of the fish until the end of time (vv. 143–44). The other two Qur'an passages considered here also mention that Jonah cried out to God from within the fish, so this is obviously an important aspect of the way Islam remembers Jonah. An important difference, however, is that the Islamic Jonah expresses repentance and remorse that is not found in the Bible. In this way, he is able to serve as a role model and reminder that God is always ready to show mercy toward those who admit their mistakes and ask for forgiveness. The biblical book ends with an intriguing question that Jonah does not answer:

> [10]Then the LORD said, "You are concerned about the bush, for which you did not labor and which you did not grow; it came into being in a night and perished in a night. [11]And should I not be concerned about Nineveh, that great city, in which there are more than a hundred and twenty thousand persons who do not know their right hand from their left, and also many animals?" (Jonah 4:10–11)

Thus, it leaves the reader to wonder if he was able to express repentance the way he does in the Qur'an.

The only other biblical book to end with a question is Nahum, which concludes by saying to Nineveh, "For who has ever escaped your endless cruelty?" (Nah 3:19). This brief poetic book either anticipates or celebrates the actual destruction of Nineveh in 612 BCE. Remembering the Assyrians for their brutality in devastating Israel, its poetry delights in Assyria's fall in a tone that echoes "Ding Dong the Witch Is Dead" in the film *The Wizard of Oz*. The links between Jonah and Nahum, with their starkly contrasting perspectives on Nineveh, would have prompted the ancient Israelite audience to reflect on the mystery of divine mercy and judgment.

Further Biblical Interpretations

The only reference to Jonah in the Hebrew Bible outside the book named after him is found in 2 Kings in a description of the reign of the Israelite King Jeroboam II, who ruled from 788 to 747 BCE: "He [Jeroboam] restored the border of Israel from Lebo-hamath as far as the Sea of the Arabah, according to the word of the LORD, the God of Israel, which he spoke by his servant Jonah son of Amittai, the prophet, who was from Gath-hepher" (2 Kgs 14:25). That the father of this Jonah and that of the prophet in the Book of Jonah (1:1) have the same name suggests the two prophets are the same person. This verse does not offer an interpretation of the Jonah tradition, and some scholars believe that the Book of Jonah might be an interpretive expansion of this verse from 2 Kings that was edited in the exilic or postexilic period (i.e., the sixth century BCE or later).

There are two references to Jonah in the New Testament that recount the same episode in Jesus's life but diverge in some interesting ways. One, from the Gospel of Luke, occurs in a passage where Jesus instructs a group of people.

> [29]When the crowds were increasing, he began to say, "This generation is an evil generation; it asks for a sign, but no sign will be given to it except the sign of Jonah. [30]For just as Jonah became a sign to the people of Nineveh, so the Son of Man will be to this generation. [31]The queen of the

South will rise at the judgment with the people of this generation and condemn them, because she came from the ends of the earth to listen to the wisdom of Solomon, and see, something greater than Solomon is here! ³²The people of Nineveh will rise up at the judgment with this generation and condemn it, because they repented at the proclamation of Jonah, and see, something greater than Jonah is here!" (Luke 11:29–32)

In this passage Jesus tells the crowds that the Son of Man (i.e., Jesus himself) will be a sign for them just as Jonah was a sign for the Ninevites. But he does not identify the nature of that sign for either his contemporaries or the people during Jonah's time. The reference to Jonah as a sign is complicated by the fact that he does not function as one in the Hebrew Bible, and that the word *sign* does not appear a single time in the Book of Jonah. Luke demonstrates familiarity with the biblical story of Jonah by mentioning that the Ninevites repented when they heard Jonah's message, and this is what sets them apart from those of Jesus's time. Luke is interpreting the earlier tradition in order to make a point about what it means that so many people of Jesus's own time did not accept his message: to say that those who rejected Jesus's message will be condemned in the final judgment by the Ninevites for failing to recognize the kind of sign Jesus offered them is a way of dramatizing the validity of Jesus's invitation to true repentance. In like manner, to say that they will be condemned by the Queen of Sheba, who recognized the wisdom of Solomon, dramatizes the value of the wisdom found in Jesus.

The other New Testament reference to Jonah is in the version of the same scene that is described in the Gospel of Matthew.

³⁸Then some of the scribes and Pharisees said to him, "Teacher, we wish to see a sign from you." ³⁹But he answered them, "An evil and adulterous generation asks for a sign, but no sign will be given to it except the sign of the prophet Jonah. ⁴⁰For just as Jonah was three days and three nights in the belly of the sea monster, so for three days and three nights the Son of Man will be in the heart of the earth. ⁴¹The people of Nineveh will rise

up at the judgment with this generation and condemn it, because they repented at the proclamation of Jonah, and see, something greater than Jonah is here! (Matt 12:38–41)

While Matthew does not mention, as does Luke, that Jonah functioned as a sign for the Ninevites, both Gospels present Jonah as a sign for those to whom Jesus preached repentance. Matthew makes the comparison to Jonah a response to the demand of the scribes and Pharisees for a sign of Jesus's authenticity—to show that he indeed comes from God. The passage makes the three days and nights that Jonah spent in the belly of the fish the basis for comparison with the duration that the Son of Man (a title applied to Jesus) will spend in the earth, a reference to the burial of Jesus. Even though the New Testament affirms that Jesus rose on the third day and so did not spend three nights in the tomb, this passage draws the early Christian audience to consider that just as Jonah emerged alive from the fish, so Jesus's resurrection from the dead answers the demand for proof of his authenticity, the divine source of his authority.

Focus for Comparison

Jonah functions as a sign in the way both the New Testament and the Qur'an interpret his story. The Gospels of both Luke and Matthew present Jonah as a sign of the validity of Jesus's message of repentance. By linking Jonah's three days in the fish with Jesus's time in the tomb, Matthew's Gospel also offers Jonah as a sign that points to Jesus's resurrection as a demonstration of his divine authority. The Qur'an presents Jonah as a sign for Muhammad, who is told to exercise patience and not be like his prophetic predecessor who cried out in distress (Q 68:48–50). By extension, the ancient Muslim audience would have understood this admonition to have patience before God to apply also to them. By referring to Jonah as a sign, these later scriptural interpretations identify Jonah in ways that go beyond the biblical account in order to invite their communities to deeper faith.

Questions to Consider

1. Are the similarities or the differences in how Jonah is presented in the Bible and the Qur'an more significant to you?

2. What is the most important way in which the Qur'an interprets the biblical Jonah story?

3. How is God's relationship with Jonah in the Qur'an similar to and different from the way it is presented in the Bible?

4. Do you think the Qur'an is successful in downplaying the idea that Jonah is a reluctant prophet?

5. Do you think Jonah is presented in a more positive light in the Qur'an than he is in the Hebrew Bible and the Old Testament? Why or why not?

6. Why might it be that the Hebrew Bible does not offer further interpretations of the Jonah tradition than the book itself?

7. What is your response to how the Gospels of Matthew and Luke interpret Jonah?

Resources for
Further Reading

For resources that are relevant primarily to one or more specific chapters of this book, the chapter numbers are given in bold and bracketed at the end of the citation.

Islam and Islamic Traditions

https://sunnah.com/. A searchable database of the hadith material. [introduction, chapter 9]

http://www.pbs.org/wgbh/sacredjourneys/content/the-hajj/. Videos and information related to the pilgrimage to Mecca. [chapter 5]

al-Kisaʾi, Muhammad ibn ʿAbd Allah. *Tales of the Prophets*. Translated by Wheeler M. Thackston Jr. Chicago: KAZI Publications, 1997. A collection of the Stories of the Prophets that dates from the twelfth century CE. [introduction, chapter 9]

El-Zein, Amira. *Islam, Arabs, and the Intelligent World of the Jinn*. Syracuse, NY: Syracuse University Press, 2009. [chapters 2, 8]

Ibn Ishaq. *The Life of Muhammad*. Translated by A. Guillaume. Oxford: Oxford University Press, 1955. The most authoritative biography of Muhammad; Ibn Ishaq died in 768.

Khalidi, Tarif. *The Muslim Jesus: Sayings and Stories in Islamic Literature*. Cambridge, MA: Harvard University Press, 2001. Includes discussion of extraqur'anic Islamic sources in which Jesus is mentioned. [chapter 1]

175

Lawson, Todd. *The Crucifixion and the Qur'an: A Study in the History of Muslim Thought*. Oxford: Oneworld, 2009. A survey of Muslim views on Jesus's death. [**chapter 1**]

Saritoprak, Zeki. *Islam's Jesus*. Gainesville: University Press of Florida, 2014. [**chapter 1**]

Schleifer, Aliah. *Mary the Blessed Virgin of Islam*. Louisville, KY: Fons Vitae, 1998. [**chapter 1**]

The Qur'an

GENERAL

Kaltner, John. *Introducing the Qur'an: For Today's Reader*. Minneapolis: Fortress Press, 2011.

Mattson, Ingrid. *The Story of the Qur'an: Its History and Place in Muslim Life*. Malden, MA: Wiley-Blackwell, 2013.

Tlili, Sarra. *Animals in the Qur'an*. Cambridge: Cambridge University Press, 2012. A treatment of both human and nonhuman animals in Islamic scripture. [**chapter 8**]

ENGLISH TRANSLATIONS

Abdel Haleem, M. A. S. *The Qur'an*. Oxford: Oxford University Press, 2004.

Droge, A. J. *The Qur'an: A New Annotated Translation*. Sheffield, UK: Equinox, 2013.

Nasr, Seyyed Hossein. *The Study Qur'an: A New Translation and Commentary*. San Francisco: HarperOne, 2015.

Comparative Studies

BROAD

Gregg, Robert C. *Shared Stories, Rival Tellings: Early Encounters of Jews, Christians, and Muslims*. Oxford: Oxford University Press, 2015. Includes an examination of the role of the Cain and Abel tradition at pages 3–74, and a treatment of Jonah at pages 408–54. [chapters 3, 10]

Kaltner, John, and Younus Y. Mirza. *The Bible and the Qur'an: Biblical Figures in the Islamic Tradition*. London: Bloomsbury T&T Clark, 2018.

Reynolds, Gabriel Said. *The Qur'an and the Bible*. New Haven, CT: Yale University Press, 2018. Identifies passages in the Qur'an that have connections with the Bible and with Jewish and Christian extrabiblical literature.

Siddiqui, Mona. *Christians, Muslims, and Jesus*. New Haven: Yale University Press, 2013. [chapter 1]

FOCUSED

George-Tvrtković, Rita. *Christians, Muslims, and Mary: A History*. New York: Paulist Press, 2018. [chapter 1]

Kvam, Kristin E., Linda S. Schearing, and Valarie H. Ziegler, eds. *Eve and Adam: Jewish, Christian, and Muslim Readings on Genesis and Gender*. Bloomington: Indiana University Press, 1999. Includes examples of misogynistic interpretations of Adam and Eve. [chapter 2]

Levenson, Jon D. *Inheriting Abraham: The Legacy of the Patriarch in Judaism, Christianity, and Islam*. Princeton, NJ: Princeton University Press, 2012. [chapter 5]

The Bible

GENERAL

Aguilar Chiu, José Enrique, Richard J. Clifford, Carol J. Dempsey, Eileen M. Schuller, Thomas Stegman, and Ronald D. Witherup, eds. *The Paulist Biblical Commentary*. New York: Paulist Press, 2018. Includes concise, accessible commentaries on each of the books of the Christian Bible along with general background articles.

Boadt, Lawrence. *Reading the Old Testament: An Introduction*. Revised by Richard Clifford and Daniel Harrington. 2nd ed. New York: Paulist Press, 2012. Offers insights concerning historical, literary, and interpretive contexts relevant to topics raised in this book.

Daniel J. Harrington. *Witnesses to the Word: New Testament Studies since Vatican II*. New York: Paulist Press, 2012. Accessible introduction to New Testament interpretation, including an annotated bibliography of recent scholarship on biblical interpretation more generally.

Perkins, Pheme. *Reading the New Testament: An Introduction*. 3rd ed. New York: Paulist Press, 2012. Includes background on numerous topics raised in this book, including New Testament titles for Jesus and the historical origins of Christianity.

DETAILED NEW TESTAMENT COMMENTARIES

Donahue, John R., and Daniel J. Harrington. *The Gospel of Mark*. Sacra Pagina 2. Collegeville, MN: Liturgical Press, 2002.

Harrington, Daniel J. *The Gospel of Matthew*. Sacra Pagina 1. Collegeville, MN: Liturgical Press, 2007.

STUDY BIBLES IN ENGLISH

Berlin, Adele, and Marc Zvi Brettler, eds. *The Jewish Study Bible*. 2nd ed. New York: Oxford University Press, 2014.

Coogan, Michael David, ed. *The New Oxford Annotated Bible: New Revised Standard Version with the Apocrypha; An Ecumenical Study Bible*. 5th ed. New York: Oxford University Press, 2018.

Senior, Donald, John J. Collins, and Mary Ann Getty, eds. *The Catholic Study Bible*. 3rd ed. New York: Oxford University Press, 2016.

SPECIAL TOPICS

Covenant

McKenzie, Steven L. *Covenant*. St. Louis: Chalice Press, 2000. [chapters 5, 6]

David and Solomon

Baden, Joel. *The Historical David: The Real Life of an Invented Hero*. San Francisco: HarperOne, 2013. Examines David's role in the Bible. [chapter 7]

Knoppers, Gary N. "Chronicles, First and Second Books of." In *The New Interpreter's Dictionary of the Bible*, edited by Katharine Doob Sakenfeld, 1:622–31. Nashville: Abingdon, 2006. [chapters 7, 8]

McKenzie, Steven L. *King David: A Biography*. Oxford: Oxford University Press, 2000. Discusses the apologetic presentation of David in the Bible. [chapter 7]

Interpretation Informed by Trauma Studies

Boase, Elizabeth, and Christopher G. Frechette, eds. *Bible through the Lens of Trauma*. Semeia Studies 86. Atlanta: SBL Press, 2016. [chapter 6]

Carr, David. *Holy Resilience: The Bible's Traumatic Origins*. New Haven, CT: Yale University Press, 2014. [chapter 6]

Frechette, Christopher G. "The Old Testament as Controlled Substance: How Insights from Trauma Studies Reveal Healing Capacities in Potentially Harmful Texts." *Interpretation: A Journal of Bible and Theology* 69 (2015): 20–34. [chapter 6]

Job and the Problem of Suffering

Levenson, Jon D. *Creation and the Persistence of Evil: The Jewish Drama of Divine Omnipotence*. Princeton, NJ: Princeton University Press, 1994. A discussion of the interplay between protest against and submission to God in the Hebrew Bible; includes detailed treatment of Job. [chapter 9]

Wisdom Literature

McLaughlin, John L. *An Introduction to Israel's Wisdom Traditions*. Grand Rapids: Eerdmans Press, 2018. [chapters 3, 8, 10]

Penchansky, David. *Understanding Wisdom Literature: Conflict and Dissonance in the Hebrew Text*. Grand Rapids: Eerdmans Press, 2012. [chapters 3, 8, 10]

Extrabiblical Jewish and Christian Sources

Barnstone, Willis. *The Other Bible: Jewish Pseudepigrapha, Christian Apocrypha, Gnostic Scriptures, Kabbalah, Dead Sea Scrolls*. Rev. ed. San Francisco: HarperSanFrancisco, 2005. Includes a brief introduction to and a translation of the Infancy Gospel of Pseudo-Matthew. [chapter 1]

Ehrman, Bart D. *Lost Scriptures: Books That Did Not Make It into the New Testament*. New York: Oxford University Press, 2003. Includes translations, with introductions, of the Proto-Gospel of James and the Infancy Gospel of Thomas. [chapter 1]

Flesher, Paul V. M., and Bruce Chilton. *The Targums: A Critical Introduction*. Waco, TX: Baylor University Press, 2011. [chapters 3, 8]

Grossfeld, Bernard. *The Two Targums of Esther*. The Aramaic Bible 18. Collegeville, MN: Liturgical Press, 1991. [chapter 8]

Jonge, Marinus de, and Johannes Tromp. *The Life of Adam and Eve and Related Literature*. Sheffield, UK: Sheffield Academic, 1997. [chapter 2]

Rubinkiewicz, R. "Apocalypse of Abraham: A New Translation and Introduction." In *The Old Testament Pseudepigrapha: Apocalyptic Literature and Testaments*, edited by James H. Charlesworth, 1:681–705. Garden City, NY: Doubleday, 1983. [chapter 5]

Wintermute, O. S. "Jubilees: A New Translation and Introduction." In Charlesworth, *Old Testament Pseudepigrapha*, 2:35–142. [chapter 5]

Notes

Introduction

1. All original-language terms provided in this book are in Arabic, unless otherwise indicated.

2. The Priestly version only describes one pair of every living thing (Gen 6:19–20), while the so-called Yahwist or J version has God ask for seven pairs of pure (i.e., ritually acceptable) animals, and one pair of impure (i.e., ritually unacceptable) animals (Gen 7:2–3). For an accessible discussion of the theological purposes of these and other differences between the two versions, see Richard J. Clifford, "Genesis," in *The Paulist Biblical Commentary*, ed. José Enrique Aguilar Chiu et al. (New York: Paulist Press, 2018), 25–28.

3. See discussions of Jesus as the Messiah in chap. 1, at pp. 15–16, 20–22, and in chap. 7, at pp. 127–28.

Chapter 1

1. The spelling of the name differs between English translations of the Bible ("Zechariah") and of the Qur'an ("Zachariah"). Since the primary focus of the discussion here is the Qur'an, for simplicity the latter spelling is used throughout this book.

2. All translations of the Qur'an in this book are by John Kaltner.

3. The term *miḥrāb* also describes an architectural feature of a mosque, the niche in a wall that identifies the direction toward Mecca that Muslims must face when they pray.

4. The Qur'an often refers to God in the first-person plural ("We," "Us," "Our"), and it is not uncommon for the text to switch between the first-person singular and plural in the same passage. This is an example of what is sometimes called the "divine we" (cf. Gen 1:26), and it does not violate the Islamic belief in God's oneness.

5. All biblical quotations are from the New Revised Standard Version.

6. Joseph is mentioned in other Muslim sources, like the collections of traditions that are known as Stories of the Prophets. In the collection by al-Kisa'i, for example, Joseph is identified as a carpenter who was Mary's cousin and took her and the newborn Jesus to Egypt when they were threatened by the Israelite king. See Muhammad ibn 'Abd Allah al-Kisa'i, *Tales of the Prophets*, trans. Wheeler M. Thackston Jr. (Chicago: KAZI Publications, 1997), 327–34.

7. In a related passage (Q 21:91) the text specifies that God breathed into "her" rather than "it."

8. Jesus makes a similar statement in Q 5:116–18, where he denies that he ever taught his followers to see him as divine.

9. See Declan Marmion and Rik Van Nieuwenhove, *An Introduction to the Trinity* (Cambridge: Cambridge University Press, 2011).

10. The stories of Jesus feeding multitudes include four basic elements of eucharistic liturgy: to take the bread, bless God for it, break it, and share it with those gathered. See, e.g., parallel accounts in Matt 14:15–21; Mark 6:35–44; and Luke 9:12–17. This pattern is also apparent in the account of the disciples who encounter Jesus in Luke 24:13–35 (discussed below).

11. In addition to the following scenes from Luke, see also Luke 6:23; 8:13; 10:17; 15:7; 15:10; Acts 8:8; 13:52; 14:17; and 15:3.

Chapter 2

1. The jinn are discussed in more detail below in chap. 8 regarding Solomon. The role of the jinn is discussed in Amira

El-Zein, *Islam, Arabs, and the Intelligent World of the Jinn* (Syracuse, NY: Syracuse University Press, 2009).

2. Additional accounts of what takes place in the garden appear in Q 2:30–39 and 15:26–50.

3. Satan actually whispers the question, and the Arabic verb for that act (*waswasa*) is a nice example of onomatopoeia that echoes the sound of whispering (cf. Q 114:1–6).

Chapter 3

1. The Arabic command "tell" is a masculine singular imperative, and this form is commonly used in the Qur'an when God directs Muhammad to communicate something to his people.

2. Diversity among ancient manuscripts containing the biblical account raises the question of whether Cain's words were quoted in the original story. However, although the received Jewish text omits them, they are preserved in many ancient versions.

3. The word *taqwā* is etymologically related, and in the Qur'an it describes the attitude of reverence and awe that marks a true believer.

4. See, e.g., Deut 6:24; Ps 112:1; Prov 19:23; Eccl 8:12–13; Isa 33:6; Luke 1:50. As discussed below in chap. 9 concerning Job, a number of biblical texts encourage a broad range of attitudes in relating to God, including honest anger and protest as well as praise and submission. The biblical concept of fearing God includes worship that can express such a full range, while the Qur'an focuses on submission. For a discussion of the biblical concept of the fear of God as related to emotionally honest worship, see Christopher G. Frechette, "'Happy Are Those Who Fear the Lord': Hope, Desire, and Transformative Worship," in *Hope: Promise, Possibility, and Fulfillment*, ed. Richard Lennan and Nancy Pineda-Madrid (New York: Paulist Press, 2013), 128–41.

5. The title "Lord of all worlds" is found, for example, in the opening chapter of the Qur'an (1:2).

6. An overview of how heaven and hell are presented in the Qur'an can be found in John Kaltner, *Introducing the Qur'an: For Today's Reader* (Minneapolis: Fortress Press, 2011), 228–42.

7. The Arabic term used here might also refer to a crow or another type of blackbird.

8. The targumic literature is a set of texts written in Aramaic that offer translations, explanations, and expansions of many passages from the Hebrew Bible.

9. In the fourth division of the Mishnah, see the section called "Sanhedrin" at 4:5.H–K.

10. The term commonly used for those works that are canonical for Catholics and Orthodox but not for other Christians is the Apocrypha.

Chapter 4

1. Additional accounts of the flood story are found in Q 7:59–64; 10:71–73; 23:23–30; 26:105–20.

2. Traditions have located Mount Judi in different areas as far away from each other as Arabia and Turkey.

3. As noted in the introduction, the biblical account shows evidence of combining two different versions of the story, each using details that may not agree with the other to communicate its own themes.

4. Extrabiblical rabbinic works contain similar scenes, and Syriac Christian sources mention that Noah preached to his contemporaries for a long period of time prior to the flood. See Gabriel Said Reynolds, *The Qur'an and the Bible* (New Haven, CT: Yale University Press, 2018), 858–59.

5. According to the Qur'an, *shirk* is the one sin that will be not forgiven by God (4:48).

6. See, e.g., Q 2:119; 5:19; 7:184, 188; 11:2, 12; 15:89; 17:105; 22:49; 25:1, 7, 56; 28:46; 29:50; 32:3; 33:45; 34:28, 46; 35:23–24; 38:70; 46:9; 48:8; 51:50–51; 53:56; 67:26.

7. Noah's words in Gen 9:25–27, the "curse of Ham," have sometimes been interpreted in ways that support racist views and practices. See Stephen R. Haynes, *Noah's Curse: The Biblical Justification of American Slavery* (Oxford: Oxford University Press, 2002).

8. Another example of this appears in Q 3:44, when an account of the angels' visit to Mary to announce the birth of Jesus

is momentarily interrupted to remind Muhammad that he was not present when the events took place.

9. The Qur'an's perspective on the family is discussed in John Kaltner, *Introducing the Qur'an: For Today's Reader* (Minneapolis: Fortress, 2011), 75–102.

10. The importance of this theme becomes apparent in the fact that God's mercy is mentioned four times in this passage (vv. 28, 41, 43, 47).

11. For more on this expectation, see Dale C. Allison, "Eschatology of the NT," in *The New Interpreter's Dictionary of the Bible*, ed. Katherine Doob Sakenfeld (Nashville: Abingdon Press, 2007), 2:294–99.

Chapter 5

1. The Arabic form of Abraham is Ibrahim, which is fairly common in the Arabic-speaking world.

2. Zoroastrianism is a religion with a monotheistic message that originated in modern-day Iran more than three thousand years ago.

3. See the discussion of the concept of association (*shirk*) in chap. 4, at pp. 67–68.

4. Some of the ways Genesis 22 can be analyzed are discussed in Bradley Beach and Matthew Powell, eds., *Interpreting Abraham: Journeys to Moriah* (Minneapolis: Fortress Press, 2014).

5. The book of Jubilees presents an alternative account of much of the Book of Genesis and was likely written in the second century BCE.

6. The other four pillars are the profession of faith, prayer, fasting, and almsgiving.

7. As discussed in the previous chapter on Noah, the latter part of the Book of Isaiah, beginning in chap. 40, reflects the situation of Israelites during the Babylonian exile and then the Persian period, which were difficult times for many of them.

8. This is a different character than the Lazarus whom Jesus raises from the dead in John 11.

Chapter 6

1. An overview of Moses's role in the Qur'an and other Islamic sources can be found in John Kaltner and Younus Y. Mirza, *The Bible and the Qur'an: Biblical Figures in the Islamic Tradition* (London: Bloomsbury T&T Clark, 2018), 125–32.

2. The first line of this description of God also appears either in full, in part, or with some variation in the following biblical texts: Pss 86:15; 103:8; 145:8; Joel 2:13; Jonah 4:2; Neh 9:17; and 2 Chr 30:9.

3. For a concise, accessible discussion of Exodus 32—34, see Christopher Frechette, "The Pentateuch [Reading Guide]," in *The Catholic Study Bible*, ed. Donald Senior, John J. Collins, and Mary Ann Getty, 3rd ed. (New York: Oxford University Press, 2016), RG145–46.

4. See the topic "Interpretation Informed by Trauma Studies" in "Resources for Further Reading."

5. This part of the story is meant to highlight the role of the priesthood since Aaron is the first priest of Israel and the tribe of Levi is designated as the priestly tribe.

6. As noted above, this Arabic term is cognate to the Hebrew term that characterizes God's self-description in Exod 34:6–7 and in multiple similar biblical passages.

7. The Qur'an interprets the mercy to be in the tablets, while Exodus attributes the mercy directly to God (Exod 34:6–7) and the tablets are replaced because they have been damaged (Exod 34:1).

8. Luke is the only other Gospel that has an infancy narrative (Luke 1—2), and it does not make a similar connection with Moses. On the Jewish character of Matthew and on Jesus as a Moses figure in it, see Daniel J. Harrington, *The Gospel of Matthew*, Sacra Pagina 1 (Collegeville, MN: Liturgical Press, 2007).

9. See, e.g., the document published by the Pontifical Biblical Commission in 2002, "The Jewish People and Their Sacred Scriptures in the Christian Bible," available at http://www.vatican.va/roman_curia/congregations/cfaith/pcb_documents/rc_con

_cfaith_doc_20020212_popolo-ebraico_en.html (accessed February 11, 2020).

Chapter 7

1. The Arabic term the Qur'an uses for the book revealed to David is *zabūr*.

2. In the Bible, the Hebrew word for the basket the infant Moses is placed in is the same as that for the ark that Noah built.

3. There are many nonqur'anic Muslim traditions about how David killed Goliath, and some are related to what is found in Jewish and Christian nonbiblical sources. According to al-Kisa'i (13th century CE), David collected stones associated with Abraham, Isaac, and Jacob and he hurled them at Goliath. One went to the left of the Philistine and another to his right, but the third struck the nosepiece of Goliath's helmet and killed him.

4. This episode is discussed in Mohammed Khaleel, *David in the Muslim Tradition: The Bathsheba Affair* (Lanham, MD: Lexington Books, 2014).

5. In this way, the Qur'an passage is an apology or defense of David that functions in a way similar to the David story in 1 Samuel, which, although it links David's abuse of his power to the punishment of his descendants, also portrays him as pious and repentant.

6. On the interpretation of Israel's history as punishment for injustice, see also the discussions of the golden calf story in chap. 6 and of Solomon in chap. 8.

7. The connection between David and the Psalms likely stems in part from the description of him as a musician who played the lyre (1 Sam 18:10–11).

8. These include Pss 3, 7, 18, 34, 51, 52, 54, 56, 57, 59, 60, 63, 142.

9. See discussions of Jesus as the Messiah in chap. 1, at pp. 15–16, 20–22, and in chap. 7, at pp. 127–28.

10. In fact, the third set (Matt 1:12–16) lists only thirteen generations.

Chapter 8

1. An overview of how Solomon is presented in the Qur'an and other Islamic sources is available in John Kaltner and Younus Y. Mirza, *The Bible and the Qur'an: Biblical Figures in the Islamic Tradition* (London: Bloomsbury T&T Clark, 2018), 160–62.

2. The lone exception is chap. 9, which does not begin with this superscription. The reason for its absence is not completely clear, but it might indicate that chaps. 8 and 9 of the Qur'an were originally one composition that was divided into two at a later point.

3. Since the two biblical versions of that story are nearly identical (1 Kgs 10:1–13; 2 Chr 9:1–12), for the sake of simplicity only parallels to the version in 1 Kings will be cited here.

4. See, e.g., 1 Kgs 2:6, 9; 3:3–14, 16–28; 4:29–34; 5:7, 12; 10:23–25; 11:41.

5. Aramaic is a Semitic language related to Hebrew; the two use the same alphabet.

6. The book is also called Ecclesiastes, its title in Greek, which translates the Hebrew title.

Chapter 9

1. The biblical Books of Psalms, Lamentations, and Jeremiah are especially rich in expressions of protest as integral to a process of relating to God with trust.

2. A similar tradition is mentioned in the Testament of Job (23.1–11), written sometime between the first century BCE and the first century CE, in which Job's wife sells her hair.

3. Another proposal suggests that the herbs or grass mentioned in this passage are part of Job's treatment to recover from his ailments.

4. See that detailed discussion, which is relevant also here, in chap. 4, at pp. 73–74.

Chapter 10

1. For instance, in his biblical prayer Jonah says nothing about being in a fish or about his time on board the ship in the previous chapter.

2. See, e.g., Q 3:200; 7:128; 16:127; 40:77; 70:5.

3. The location of Tarshish is not completely certain, but it was likely Tartessos on the Iberian Peninsula.

4. The Qur'an adds the detail that Jonah was ill when he was returned to dry land (v. 145).

5. The Hebrew verb *mānāh* ("to appoint") is a key word in the biblical account that is also used to describe how God sends the fish in 1:17.

Scripture Index